D1187850

COLLINS
ANNOTATED STUDENT TEXTS

General Editor

MARK ROBERTS
Professor of English
The Queen's University of Belfast

COLLINS ANNOTATED STUDENT TEXTS

Available

TENNYSON: POEMS OF 1842: ed. Christopher Ricks
WORDSWORTH AND COLERIDGE: LYRICAL BALLADS: ed. D. S. Roper
BROWNING: DRAMATIS PERSONAE: ed. F. B. Pinion
HAZLITT: THE SPIRIT OF THE AGE: ed. E. D. Mackerness
KEATS: POEMS OF 1820: ed. Professor D. G. Gillham
BYRON: DON JUAN (1819): ed. Brian Lee

In preparation

RUSKIN: UNTO THIS LAST: ed. P. M. Yarker
BLAKE: POEMS FROM THE ROSSETTI MS: ed. R. B. Kennedy
POPE: ESSAY ON CRITICISM; THE RAPE OF THE LOCK; MORAL
  ESSAYS: ed. R. G. T. Southall
JOHNSON: LONDON; VANITY OF HUMAN WISHES; PREFACE TO
  SHAKESPEARE; RASSELAS; REVIEW OF AN ENQUIRY INTO THE
  ORIGIN AND NATURE OF EVIL
DRYDEN: ABSALOM AND ACHITOPHEL; THE MEDAL; MACFLECKNOE;
  RELIGIO LAICI: ed. Philip Roberts
MILTON: POEMS OF 1645: ed. Brian Nellist
CONGREVE: THE DOUBLE DEALER; LOVE FOR LOVE; THE WAY OF
  THE WORLD: ed. R. N. G. Salgado
CRABBE: THE VILLAGE; THE PARISH REGISTER: ed. F. B. Pinion
SHELLEY: ALASTOR AND OTHER POEMS; PROMETHEUS UNBOUND;
  ADONAIS: ed. Professor P. H. Butter
BROWNING: MEN AND WOMEN: ed. Professor G. Bullough
EDWARD THOMAS: POEMS (1917); LAST POEMS (1918): ed. Edna
  Longley

JOHN KEATS

Poems of 1820

and

The Fall of Hyperion

Edited by

D. G. GILLHAM, M.A., Ph.D.

Professor of English
University of Natal

COLLINS PUBLISHERS: LONDON AND GLASGOW

First published 1969

Printed in Great Britain
Collins Clear-Type Press

General Preface

This series has two principal aims:
1. To meet the needs of both sixth-formers and under-graduates;
2. To encourage the student to *read the text* of the author he is studying rather than have recourse to substitutes which will tell him (as he hopes) 'what he ought to think.'

The annotation, accordingly, is designed as a tool with which to read the text. The conventional introduction has been eliminated and is replaced by a brief preface indicating the principal topics that scholars and critics discuss in connection with an author's work.

Authors are not represented in this series by volumes of selections of the kind that is now so familiar. Selections are in any case of limited use to the serious student. But there is the further point that in a volume of selections the pieces selected and the context they create for other pieces exercise a great influence upon the reader's impression of the author. When the present series was planned, it was felt that it would be much better to choose from an author's work, not individual pieces, but what are by common consent key *volumes*, so that each piece might appear in its original context. In this way, the overall impression of each volume is put firmly back in the hands of its author.

Editors have been asked to produce 'standard' texts on conventional lines, and the text of a poem in one of these volumes, therefore, will normally be that which the reader is most likely to meet in other contexts. Each editor, however, has been given a wide measure of freedom to make what seems to him the most sensible decision in the case of his own particular text, and the textual status of each volume is fully described in the Note on the Text with which it begins. In addition, important variants are recorded in the Notes.

MARK ROBERTS

Contents

Acknowledgments

The Editors and Publishers desire to make grateful acknowledgment to the following for permission to include copyright material as stated:

Chatto and Windus Ltd. for the extracts from *Revaluation* by F. R. Leavis;

Chatto and Windus Ltd. and New Directions Publishing Corporation, New York (all rights reserved) for the extract from *Seven Types of Ambiguity* by William Empson;

The Clarendon Press, Oxford, for the extracts from *The Poetical Works of John Keats* by H. W. Garrod, *Keats' Craftsmanship* by M. R. Ridley, and *Collected Essays* (vol. IV) by Robert Bridges;

Dennis Dobson (Publishers) for the extract from *The Well Wrought Urn* by Cleanth Brooks;

Faber and Faber Ltd., and Harcourt, Brace and World, Inc., New York, for the extract from 'Tradition and the Individual Talent' from *Selected Essays* by T. S. Eliot;

Farrar, Straus and Giroux, Inc., New York, for the extract from the Introduction to *Selected Letters of John Keats* by Lionel Trilling;

Liverpool University Press for the extracts from *John Keats; A Reassessment* by Kenneth Muir;

Macmillan and Co. Ltd. for the extracts from *John Keats: His Life and Poetry, His Friends, Critics and After-Fame* by Sir Sidney Colvin;

Methuen and Co. Ltd. for the extract from *The Starlit Dome* by G. Wilson Knight;

The Society of Authors as the literary representative of the Estate of John Middleton Murry for the extracts from *Keats and Shakespeare* and *Studies in Keats* by J. M. Murry;

University of Toronto Press for the extract from *Keats: A Bibliography and Reference Guide* by J. R. Macgillivray;

The University of Virginia for the extract from *Studies in Bibliography* by Jack Stillinger.

Note on the Text
of this Edition

THIS VOLUME contains the poems published by Keats in 1820, with the addition of *The Fall of Hyperion* (Keats's revision of *Hyperion: A Fragment*). The text of the 1820 volume has been reproduced except in one or two places where, for the sake of consistency, initial capitals have been added to words. These alterations are remarked on in the notes. Disparities between the 1820 volume and Keats's manuscript version are also noted where they are of particular significance. The poems of 1820 were originally entitled: *Lamia, Isabella, The Eve of St. Agnes, and Other Poems, by John Keats, Author of Endymion*. The Advertisement which appeared at the beginning of the volume was supplied by the publishers, and reads:

> If any apology be thought necessary for the appearance of the unfinished poem of HYPERION, the publishers beg to state that they alone are responsible, as it was printed at their particular request, and contrary to the wish of the author. The poem was intended to have been of equal length with ENDYMION, but the reception given to that work discouraged the author from proceeding.
>
> (*Fleet-Street, June 26, 1820*)

Keats crossed this advertisement out in one copy of the book, and wrote: 'This is none of my doing—I was ill at the time.' Beneath the last sentence he wrote: 'This is a lie.'

Keats never published *The Fall of Hyperion*, but it seems right that it should be included in a volume that contains the Odes and the original fragment of *Hyperion*.

The two *Hyperions* form a contrast and they illuminate each other. In the Odes and *The Fall of Hyperion* Keats reached the height of his powers, and the inclusion of these poems in the same volume allows them to be studied together. The version of *The Fall of Hyperion* printed here corresponds to the copy of the poem made by Keats's friend, Richard Woodhouse, since the original manuscript is now lost. The capitalization, which is irregular, has been altered to correspond with Keats's usage in the earlier *Hyperion*, and one or two full stops have been added (and noted).

The quotations from Keats's letters in the Notes and in the Critical Extracts at the end of the volume are given as he wrote them, though they were sometimes hastily written and require punctuation.

Prefatory Note

KEATS'S SHORT WORKING life as a poet was limited to the three years between July 1816, when he left Guy's Hospital, and the end of 1819, when he became seriously ill. He composed all his important verse during this period, before reaching the age of 24, and at 25 he died of consumption after a lingering and distressing illness. He was always beset by financial anxieties, and the illness and death of his brother Tom, his concern for George and Fanny Keats, and his own poor health all added to the strain of his life. In spite of adverse circumstances he made rapid progress as a poet, published three volumes of poetry, composed much verse not published in his lifetime, and wrote the remarkable letters, now almost as famous as the poems. Keats's best poetry is contained in his last volume, published in 1820, and in his revision of *Hyperion*, both of which are reproduced here. He wrote these poems in 1818 and 1819, they are more mature than his previous work, and Keats continued to develop as a poet as he composed them.

We have a great deal of information about Keats's life. His letters are detailed and his friends, recognizing his genius, preserved his miscellaneous fragments and papers. Keats's first biographer, R. Monckton Milnes, was able to consult persons who had known Keats intimately, and later research has brought much additional material to light.

All Keats's work shows his rich gift for musical and sensuous expression, and many of his critics have seen little else to admire (or to dislike) in his verse. Keats's detractors in the 1820s regarded this quality as effeminate, and Keats's reputation suffered further as a result of the story put about by Shelley, who was abetted by Byron and many of Keats's friends, that the poet had died of grief at the adverse criticism directed at him in *Blackwood's Edinburgh Magazine* and *The Quarterly Review* (see Critical Extracts, pp. 204-5). It was not until Milnes issued his *Life, Letters and Literary Remains* (see Bibliography, p. 219) in 1848 that Keats's 'milk and water' reputation began to fade. During the nineteenth century too much emphasis was probably laid on Keats's 'verbal magic.' Lamb praised him extravagantly for it. Tennyson and Swinburne imitated him. D. G. Rossetti and the Pre-Raphaelites were enraptured by Keats, particularly by the works that most enchantingly lead the mind into a world of fantasy: *The Eve of St. Agnes, Isabella* and *La Belle Dame Sans Merci* (written at the same time as the Odes but omitted from the 1820 *Poems*). Pater proclaimed that Keats realized the principle of Art for its own sake. On the whole the uncritical acceptance of Keats as the prophet of Beauty has done his reputation more harm than good, however, and the analysis of his style and imagery by modern critics like G. Wilson Knight and W. J. Bate does justice to the poet in a way that no amount of inert acceptance could do. The reader who supposes that *Lamia*, for example, because it contains some enchanting descriptions is successful in all respects has probably not given the poem the attention due to it.

During the last forty years critical attention has tended to focus, if not exactly on Keats's 'philosophy,' then on the mind behind the poetry, on Keats's conscious or unconscious purpose. The narrative poems have given way in importance to the letters, where Keats's ambitions as a poet are clearly stated, and to *The Fall of Hyperion*, which makes its statement in symbolic form. The critics are engaged in 'making sense' of Keats, though without attributing any dogma to him. Keats's poetry resists any rigidly theoretical interpretation, and in his letters, where he describes his aims with much insight, he defines the poet as a man who is sensitive rather than one who interprets, one whose knowledge is of the 'heart' rather than of the 'mind.' As T. S. Eliot says, Keats had a 'shrewd and penetrating intellect,' but 'Keats has no theory, and to have formed one was irrelevant to his interests, and alien to his mind.' Matthew Arnold set the tone for much good Keats criticism when he pointed out that, though Keats was passionately devoted to the 'beautiful,' he did not surrender his strength and spirit to it (see Critical Extracts, p. 211). It is the vigorous personality of the poet and not any set of abstract ideas or any didactic purpose which lends firmness to his verse. Keats's bent is aesthetic, but he is no relaxed 'aesthete.' For him, the encounter with Beauty was a way of meeting experience, not avoiding it, and in his best poetry (in *The Eve of St. Agnes*, the *Ode to a Nightingale* and *Ode on a Grecian Urn*, for example) Keats has one eye on a world of enchantment, the other on the common earth. F. R. Leavis says: 'We can see why Pre-Raphaelite and Aesthete should have looked to Keats as they did: we can ourselves see in Keats (if we can see more too) the great Aesthete—the one Aesthete of genius.' And in discussing the *Ode on Melancholy* Leavis shows how the 'voluptuary's itch to be fingering,' associated with Keats, is indicative, also, of a 'strong grasp upon actualities' which is 'at once intelligence and character.'

Principal Dates of Keats's Life

1795   John Keats born 31 October at the livery stables attached to the 'Swan and Hoop', Finsbury, London. [Keats's brothers George and Tom were born in 1797 and 1799; his sister Fanny in 1803.]

1803–11   Attends the school at Enfield conducted by John Clarke. Commences friendship with Charles Cowden Clarke. His father dies in 1804; his mother (who had remarried) in 1810; and his surviving grandmother, Alice Jennings, in 1814.

1811–15   Apprenticed to Thomas Hammond, a surgeon, at Edmonton, and writes his first poems.

1815   Enters Guy's Hospital as a student.

1816   *5 May*: First poem to be published appears in Leigh Hunt's *Examiner*.

    July: Becomes licensed to practise as surgeon and apothecary but decides to try his fortune as a poet.

    October: Meets Leigh Hunt and Benjamin Robert Haydon (the painter) who encourage him.

    December: Makes the acquaintance of Shelley.

    In 1816–17 establishes his circle of friends (all men): Mathew, Haslam, Severn, Reynolds, Bailey, Rice, Dilke, Brown, Woodhouse, Taylor.

1817   *January*: Completes the volume of *Poems* published by C. & J. Ollier in March.

    March: Moves, with his brothers, into rooms at Well Walk, Hampstead.

    April-May: Works on *Endymion* in the Isle of Wight and at Margate.

    September: At Oxford with Bailey.

    November: Completes *Endymion*.

    December: Introduced to Wordsworth.

1818   *January*: Writes *Lines on the Mermaid Tavern* and *Robin Hood*.

    March-April: Writes *Isabella* at Teignmouth.

    April: *Endymion* published by Taylor & Hessey. Adversely reviewed in *The Quarterly Review* (April), by John Wilson Croker, a Tory politician and devotee of

Pope, and in *Blackwood's Edinburgh Magazine* (August), probably by John Gibson Lockhart, another Tory, Sir Walter Scott's son-in-law.

June: Sees his brother George off to America and proceeds to Scotland with Charles Brown on a walking tour.

August: Returns to London to find his youngest brother, Tom, seriously ill.

September-November: Nurses Tom, who dies of consumption on 1 December. Composes most of *Hyperion*. Meets Fanny Brawne.

December: Moves into Wentworth Place, Hampstead, the home of Charles Brown. (This house is now preserved as the Keats Museum.) Writes *Fancy* and *Bards of Passion and of Mirth*.

1819 *January*: Writes *The Eve of St. Agnes*.

April-May: Writes *Ode to Psyche*, *Ode to a Nightingale*, *Ode on a Grecian Urn*, and *Ode on Melancholy*.

11 *April*: Chance meeting with Coleridge on Hampstead Heath.

July-September: In the Isle of Wight and at Winchester. Writes *Lamia*, a revised version of *Hyperion* entitled *The Fall of Hyperion*, and the Ode *To Autumn*.

October-December: At Wentworth Place, in poor health owing to tuberculosis of the lungs entering an active stage. Becomes engaged to Fanny Brawne.

1820 *February*: A haemorrhage of the lungs proves to him the nature of his illness.

June-September: Cared for by the Hunts and the Brawnes. *Lamia, Isabella, The Eve of St. Agnes, and Other Poems* (now known as the Poems of 1820) published in July by Taylor & Hessey.

September: Sails for Italy with Joseph Severn as companion.

1821 23 *February*: Dies of consumption at Rome, aged 25, and is buried in the Protestant Cemetery. On his tombstone appear the words of his self-composed epitaph: 'Here lies one whose name was writ in water.'

June: Shelley publishes *Adonais*, an elegy on the death of Keats.

Poems of 1820

LAMIA

PART I

UPON a time, before the faery broods
Drove Nymph and Satyr from the prosperous woods,
Before King Oberon's bright diadem,
Sceptre, and mantle, clasp'd with dewy gem,
Frighted away the Dryads and the Fauns   5
From rushes green, and brakes, and cowslip'd lawns,
The ever-smitten Hermes empty left
His golden throne, bent warm on amorous theft:
From high Olympus had he stolen light,
On this side of Jove's clouds, to escape the sight   10
Of his great summoner, and made retreat
Into a forest on the shores of Crete.
For somewhere in that sacred island dwelt
A nymph, to whom all hoofed Satyrs knelt;
At whose white feet the languid Tritons poured   15
Pearls, while on land they wither'd and adored.
Fast by the springs where she to bathe was wont,
And in those meads where sometime she might haunt,
Were strewn rich gifts, unknown to any Muse,
Though Fancy's casket were unlock'd to choose.   20
Ah, what a world of love was at her feet!
So Hermes thought, and a celestial heat
Burnt from his winged heels to either ear,
That from a whiteness, as the lily clear,
Blush'd into roses 'mid his golden hair,   25
Fallen in jealous curls about his shoulders bare.
From vale to vale, from wood to wood, he flew,
Breathing upon the flowers his passion new,
And wound with many a river to its head,

To find where this sweet nymph prepar'd her   30
 secret bed:
In vain; the sweet nymph might nowhere be found,
And so he rested, on the lonely ground,
Pensive, and full of painful jealousies
Of the Wood-Gods, and even the very trees.
There as he stood, he heard a mournful voice,   35
Such as once heard, in gentle heart, destroys
All pain but pity: thus the lone voice spake:
'When from this wreathed tomb shall I awake!
'When move in a sweet body fit for life,
'And love, and pleasure, and the ruddy strife   40
'Of hearts and lips! Ah, miserable me!'
The God, dove-footed, glided silently
Round bush and tree, soft-brushing, in his speed,
The taller grasses and full-flowering weed,
Until he found a palpitating snake,   45
Bright, and cirque-couchant in a dusky brake.

 She was a gordian shape of dazzling hue,
Vermilion-spotted, golden, green, and blue;
Striped like a zebra, freckled like a pard,
Eyed like a peacock, and all crimson barr'd;   50
And full of silver moons, that, as she breathed,
Dissolv'd, or brighter shone, or interwreathed
Their lustres with the gloomier tapestries—
So rainbow-sided, touch'd with miseries,
She seem'd, at once, some penanced lady elf,   55
Some demon's mistress, or the demon's self.
Upon her crest she wore a wannish fire
Sprinkled with stars, like Ariadne's tiar:
Her head was serpent, but ah, bitter-sweet!
She had a woman's mouth with all its pearls   60
 complete:
And for her eyes: what could such eyes do there
But weep, and weep, that they were born so fair?

As Proserpine still weeps for her Sicilian air.
Her throat was serpent, but the words she spake
Came, as through bubbling honey, for Love's sake,   65
And thus; while Hermes on his pinions lay,
Like a stoop'd falcon ere he takes his prey.

  'Fair Hermes, crown'd with feathers, fluttering
    light,
'I had a splendid dream of thee last night:
'I saw thee sitting, on a throne of gold,   70
'Among the Gods, upon Olympus old,
'The only sad one; for thou didst not hear
'The soft, lute-finger'd Muses chaunting clear,
'Nor even Apollo when he sang alone,
'Deaf to his throbbing throat's long, long melodious   75
    moan.
'I dreamt I saw thee, robed in purple flakes,
'Break amorous through the clouds, as morning
    breaks,
'And, swiftly as a bright Phœbean dart,
'Strike for the Cretan isle; and here thou art!
'Too gentle Hermes, hast thou found the maid?'   80
Whereat the star of Lethe not delay'd
His rosy eloquence, and thus inquired:
'Thou smooth-lipp'd serpent, surely high inspired!
'Thou beauteous wreath, with melancholy eyes,
'Possess whatever bliss thou canst devise,   85
'Telling me only where my nymph is fled,—
'Where she doth breathe!' 'Bright planet, thou hast
    said,'
Return'd the snake, 'but seal with oaths, fair God!'
'I swear,' said Hermes, 'by my serpent rod,
'And by thine eyes, and by thy starry crown!'   90
Light flew his earnest words, among the blossoms
    blown.
Then thus again the brilliance feminine:

'Too frail of heart! for this lost nymph of thine,
'Free as the air, invisibly, she strays
'About these thornless wilds; her pleasant days   95
'She tastes unseen; unseen her nimble feet
'Leave traces in the grass and flowers sweet;
'From weary tendrils, and bow'd branches green,
'She plucks the fruit unseen, she bathes unseen:
'And by my power is her beauty veil'd   100
'To keep it unaffronted, unassail'd
'By the love-glances of unlovely eyes,
'Of Satyrs, Fauns, and blear'd Silenus' sighs.
'Pale grew her immortality, for woe
'Of all these lovers, and she grieved so   105
'I took compassion on her, bade her steep
'Her hair in weïrd syrops, that would keep
'Her loveliness invisible, yet free
'To wander as she loves, in liberty.
'Thou shalt behold her, Hermes, thou alone,   110
'If thou wilt, as thou swearest, grant my boon!'
Then, once again, the charmed God began
An oath, and through the serpent's ears it ran
Warm, tremulous, devout, psalterian.
Ravish'd, she lifted her Circean head,   115
Blush'd a live damask, and swift-lisping said,
'I was a woman, let me have once more
'A woman's shape, and charming as before.
'I love a youth of Corinth—O the bliss!
'Give me my woman's form, and place me where   120
      he is.
'Stoop, Hermes, let me breathe upon thy brow,
'And thou shalt see thy sweet nymph even now.'
The God on half-shut feathers sank serene,
She breath'd upon his eyes, and swift was seen
Of both the guarded nymph near-smiling on the   125
      green.
It was no dream; or say a dream it was,

21

Real are the dreams of Gods, and smoothly pass
Their pleasures in a long immortal dream.
One warm, flush'd moment, hovering, it might seem
Dash'd by the wood-nymph's beauty, so he burn'd;   130
Then, lighting on the printless verdure, turn'd
To the swoon'd serpent, and with languid arm,
Delicate, put to proof the lythe Caducean charm.
So done, upon the nymph his eyes he bent
Full of adoring tears and blandishment,   135
And towards her stept: she, like a moon in wane,
Faded before him, cower'd, nor could restrain
Her fearful sobs, self-folding like a flower
That faints into itself at evening hour:
But the God fostering her chilled hand,   140
She felt the warmth, her eyelids open'd bland,
And, like new flowers at morning song of bees,
Bloom'd, and gave up her honey to the lees.
Into the green-recessed woods they flew;
Nor grew they pale, as mortal lovers do.   145

   Left to herself, the serpent now began
To change; her elfin blood in madness ran,
Her mouth foam'd, and the grass, therewith besprent,
Wither'd at dew so sweet and virulent;
Her eyes in torture fix'd, and anguish drear,   150
Hot, glaz'd, and wide, with lid-lashes all sear,
Flash'd phosphor and sharp sparks, without one
   cooling tear.
The colours all inflam'd throughout her train,
She writh'd about, convuls'd with scarlet pain:
A deep volcanian yellow took the place   155
Of all her milder-mooned body's grace;
And, as the lava ravishes the mead,
Spoilt all her silver mail, and golden brede;
Made gloom of all her frecklings, streaks and bars,
Eclips'd her crescents, and lick'd up her stars: 160

So that, in moments few, she was undrest
Of all her sapphires, greens, and amethyst,
And rubious-argent: of all these bereft,
Nothing but pain and ugliness were left.
Still shone her crown; that vanish'd, also she   165
Melted and disappear'd as suddenly;
And in the air, her new voice luting soft,
Cried, 'Lycius! gentle Lycius!'—Borne aloft
With the bright mists about the mountains hoar
These words dissolv'd: Crete's forests heard no more. 170

    Whither fled Lamia, now a lady bright,
A full-born beauty new and exquisite?
She fled into that valley they pass o'er
Who go to Corinth from Cenchreas' shore;
And rested at the foot of those wild hills,   175
The rugged founts of the Peræan rills,
And of that other ridge whose barren back
Stretches, with all its mist and cloudy rack,
South-westward to Cleone. There she stood
About a young bird's flutter from a wood,   180
Fair, on a sloping green of mossy tread,
By a clear pool, wherein she passioned
To see herself escap'd from so sore ills,
While her robes flaunted with the daffodils.

    Ah, happy Lycius!—for she was a maid   185
More beautiful than ever twisted braid,
Or sigh'd, or blush'd, or on spring-flowered lea
Spread a green kirtle to the minstrelsy:
A virgin purest lipp'd, yet in the lore
Of love deep learned to the red heart's core: 190
Not one hour old, yet of sciential brain
To unperplex bliss from its neighbour pain;
Define their pettish limits, and estrange
Their points of contact, and swift counterchange;

23

Intrigue with the specious chaos, and dispart 195
Its most ambiguous atoms with sure art;
As though in Cupid's college she had spent
Sweet days a lovely graduate, still unshent,
And kept his rosy terms in idle languishment.

Why this fair creature chose so fairily 200
By the wayside to linger, we shall see;
But first 'tis fit to tell how she could muse
And dream, when in the serpent prison-house,
Of all she list, strange or magnificent:
How, ever, where she will'd, her spirit went; 205
Whether to faint Elysium, or where
Down through tress-lifting waves the Nereids fair
Wind into Thetis' bower by many a pearly stair;
Or where God Bacchus drains his cups divine,
Stretch'd out, at ease, beneath a glutinous pine; 210
Or where in Pluto's gardens palatine
Mulciber's columns gleam in far piazzian line.
And sometimes into cities she would send
Her dream, with feast and rioting to blend;
And once, while among mortals dreaming thus, 215
She saw the young Corinthian Lycius
Charioting foremost in the envious race,
Like a young Jove with calm uneager face,
And fell into a swooning love of him.
Now on the moth-time of that evening dim 220
He would return that way, as well she knew,
To Corinth from the shore; for freshly blew
The eastern soft wind, and his galley now
Grated the quaystones with her brazen prow
In port Cenchreas, from Egina isle 225
Fresh anchor'd; whither he had been awhile
To sacrifice to Jove, whose temple there
Waits with high marble doors for blood and incense
        rare.

Jove heard his vows, and better'd his desire;
For by some freakful chance he made retire   230
From his companions, and set forth to walk,
Perhaps grown wearied of their Corinth talk:
Over the solitary hills he fared,
Thoughtless at first, but ere eve's star appeared
His phantasy was lost, where reason fades,   235
In the calm'd twilight of Platonic shades.
Lamia beheld him coming, near, more near—
Close to her passing, in indifference drear,
His silent sandals swept the mossy green;
So neighbour'd to him, and yet so unseen   240
She stood: he pass'd, shut up in mysteries,
His mind wrapp'd like his mantle, while her eyes
Follow'd his steps, and her neck regal white
Turn'd—syllabling thus, 'Ah, Lycius bright,
'And will you leave me on the hills alone?   245
'Lycius, look back! and be some pity shown.'
He did; not with cold wonder fearingly,
But Orpheus-like at an Eurydice;
For so delicious were the words she sung,
It seem'd he had lov'd them a whole summer long: 250
And soon his eyes had drunk her beauty up,
Leaving no drop in the bewildering cup,
And still the cup was full,—while he, afraid
Lest she should vanish ere his lip had paid
Due adoration, thus began to adore;   255
Her soft look growing coy, she saw his chain so sure:
'Leave thee alone! Look back! Ah, Goddess, see
'Whether my eyes can ever turn from thee!
'For pity do not this sad heart belie—
'Even as thou vanishest so I shall die.   260
'Stay! though a Naiad of the rivers, stay!
'To thy far wishes will thy streams obey:
'Stay! though the greenest woods be thy domain,
'Alone they can drink up the morning rain:

25

'Though a descended Pleiad, will not one   265
'Of thine harmonious sisters keep in tune
'Thy spheres, and as thy silver proxy shine?
'So sweetly to these ravish'd ears of mine
'Came thy sweet greeting, that if thou shouldst fade
'Thy memory will waste me to a shade:—   270
'For pity do not melt!'—'If I should stay,'
Said Lamia, 'here, upon this floor of clay,
'And pain my steps upon these flowers too rough,
'What canst thou say or do of charm enough
'To dull the nice remembrance of my home?   275
'Thou canst not ask me with thee here to roam
'Over these hills and vales, where no joy is,—
'Empty of immortality and bliss!
'Thou art a scholar, Lycius, and must know
'That finer spirits cannot breathe below   280
'In human climes, and live: Alas! poor youth,
'What taste of purer air hast thou to soothe
'My essence? What serener palaces,
'Where I may all my many senses please,
'And by mysterious sleights a hundred thirsts   285
    appease?
'It cannot be—Adieu!' So said, she rose
Tiptoe with white arms spread. He, sick to lose
The amorous promise of her lone complain,
Swoon'd, murmuring of love, and pale with pain.
The cruel lady, without any show   290
Of sorrow for her tender favourite's woe,
But rather, if her eyes could brighter be,
With brighter eyes and slow amenity,
Put her new lips to his, and gave afresh
The life she had so tangled in her mesh: 295
And as he from one trance was wakening
Into another, she began to sing,
Happy in beauty, life, and love, and every thing,
A song of love, too sweet for earthly lyres,

While, like held breath, the stars drew in their   300
    panting fires.
And then she whisper'd in such trembling tone,
As those who, safe together met alone
For the first time through many anguish'd days,
Use other speech than looks; bidding him raise
His drooping head, and clear his soul of doubt,   305
For that she was a woman, and without
Any more subtle fluid in her veins
Than throbbing blood, and that the self-same pains
Inhabited her frail-strung heart as his.
And next she wonder'd how his eyes could miss   310
Her face so long in Corinth, where, she said,
She dwelt but half retir'd, and there had led
Days happy as the gold coin could invent
Without the aid of love; yet in content
Till she saw him, as once she pass'd him by,   315
Where 'gainst a column he leant thoughtfully
At Venus' temple porch, 'mid baskets heap'd
Of amorous herbs and flowers, newly reap'd
Late on that eve, as 'twas the night before
The Adonian feast; whereof she saw no more,   320
But wept alone those days, for why should she adore?
Lycius from death awoke into amaze,
To see her still, and singing so sweet lays;
Then from amaze into delight he fell
To hear her whisper woman's lore so well;   325
And every word she spake entic'd him on
To unperplex'd delight and pleasure known.
Let the mad poets say whate'er they please
Of the sweets of Fairies, Peris, Goddesses,
There is not such a treat among them all,   330
Haunters of cavern, lake, and waterfall,
As a real woman, lineal indeed
From Pyrrha's pebbles or old Adam's seed.
Thus gentle Lamia judg'd, and judg'd aright,

That Lycius could not love in half a fright,   335
So threw the goddess off, and won his heart
More pleasantly by playing woman's part,
With no more awe than what her beauty gave,
That, while it smote, still guaranteed to save.
Lycius to all made eloquent reply,   340
Marrying to every word a twinborn sigh;
And last, pointing to Corinth, ask'd her sweet,
If 'twas too far that night for her soft feet.
The way was short, for Lamia's eagerness
Made, by a spell, the triple league decrease   345
To a few paces; not at all surmised
By blinded Lycius, so in her comprized.
They pass'd the city gates, he knew not how,
So noiseless, and he never thought to know.

As men talk in a dream, so Corinth all,   350
Throughout her palaces imperial,
And all her populous streets and temples lewd,
Mutter'd, like tempest in the distance brew'd,
To the wide-spreaded night above her towers.
Men, women, rich and poor, in the cool hours,   355
Shuffled their sandals o'er the pavement white,
Companion'd or alone; while many a light
Flared, here and there, from wealthy festivals,
And threw their moving shadows on the walls,
Or found them cluster'd in the corniced shade   360
Of some arch'd temple door, or dusky colonnade.

Muffling his face, of greeting friends in fear,
Her fingers he press'd hard, as one came near
With curl'd gray beard, sharp eyes, and smooth bald
    crown,
Slow-stepp'd, and robed in philosophic gown: 365
Lycius shrank closer, as they met and past,
Into his mantle, adding wings to haste,

While hurried Lamia trembled: 'Ah,' said he,
'Why do you shudder, love, so ruefully?
'Why does your tender palm dissolve in dew?'—   370
'I'm wearied,' said fair Lamia: 'tell me who
'Is that old man? I cannot bring to mind
'His features:—Lycius! wherefore did you blind
'Yourself from his quick eyes?' Lycius replied,
"Tis Apollonius sage, my trusty guide   375
'And good instructor; but to-night he seems
'The ghost of folly haunting my sweet dreams.'

    While yet he spake they had arrived before
A pillar'd porch, with lofty portal door,
Where hung a silver lamp, whose phosphor glow   380
Reflected in the slabbed steps below,
Mild as a star in water; for so new,
And so unsullied was the marble hue,
So through the crystal polish, liquid fine,
Ran the dark veins, that none but feet divine   385
Could e'er have touch'd there. Sounds Æolian
Breath'd from the hinges, as the ample span
Of the wide doors disclos'd a place unknown
Some time to any, but those two alone,
And a few Persian mutes, who that same year   390
Were seen about the markets: none knew where
They could inhabit; the most curious
Were foil'd, who watch'd to trace them to their house:
And but the flitter-winged verse must tell,
For truth's sake, what woe afterwards befel,   395
'Twould humour many a heart to leave them thus,
Shut from the busy world of more incredulous.

PART II

LOVE in a hut, with water and a crust,
Is—Love, forgive us!—cinders, ashes, dust;
Love in a palace is perhaps at last
More grievous torment than a hermit's fast:—
That is a doubtful tale from faery land,   5
Hard for the non-elect to understand.
Had Lycius liv'd to hand his story down,
He might have given the moral a fresh frown,
Or clench'd it quite: but too short was their bliss
To breed distrust and hate, that make the soft   10
    voice hiss.
Besides, there, nightly, with terrific glare,
Love, jealous grown of so complete a pair,
Hover'd and buzz'd his wings, with fearful roar,
Above the lintel of their chamber door,
And down the passage cast a glow upon the floor.   15

    For all this came a ruin: side by side
They were enthroned, in the even tide,
Upon a couch, near to a curtaining
Whose airy texture, from a golden string,
Floated into the room, and let appear   20
Unveil'd the summer heaven, blue and clear,
Betwixt two marble shafts:—there they reposed,
Where use had made it sweet, with eyelids closed,
Saving a tythe which love still open kept,
That they might see each other while they almost   25
    slept;
When from the slope side of a suburb hill,
Deafening the swallow's twitter, came a thrill
Of trumpets—Lycius started—the sounds fled,
But left a thought, a buzzing in his head.
For the first time, since first he harbour'd in   30
That purple-lined palace of sweet sin,

His spirit pass'd beyond its golden bourn
Into the noisy world almost forsworn.
The lady, ever watchful, penetrant,
Saw this with pain, so arguing a want   35
Of something more, more than her empery
Of joys; and she began to moan and sigh
Because he mused beyond her, knowing well
That but a moment's thought is passion's passing
    bell.
'Why do you sigh, fair creature?' whisper'd he: 40
'Why do you think?' return'd she tenderly:
'You have deserted me;—where am I now?
'Not in your heart while care weighs on your brow:
'No, no, you have dismiss'd me; and I go
'From your breast houseless: ay, it must be so.'   45
He answer'd, bending to her open eyes,
Where he was mirror'd small in paradise,
'My silver planet, both of eve and morn!
'Why will you plead yourself so sad forlorn,
'While I am striving how to fill my heart   50
'With deeper crimson, and a double smart?
'How to entangle, trammel up and snare
'Your soul in mine, and labyrinth you there
'Like the hid scent in an unbudded rose?
'Ay, a sweet kiss—you see your mighty woes.   55
'My thoughts! shall I unveil them? Listen then!
'What mortal hath a prize, that other men
'May be confounded and abash'd withal,
'But lets it sometimes pace abroad majestical,
'And triumph, as in thee I should rejoice   60
'Amid the hoarse alarm of Corinth's voice.
'Let my foes choke, and my friends shout afar,
'While through the thronged streets your bridal car
'Wheels round its dazzling spokes.'—The lady's
    cheek
Trembled; she nothing said, but, pale and meek,   65

31

Arose and knelt before him, wept a rain
Of sorrows at his words; at last with pain
Beseeching him, the while his hand she wrung,
To change his purpose. He thereat was stung,
Perverse, with stronger fancy to reclaim   70
Her wild and timid nature to his aim:
Besides, for all his love, in self despite,
Against his better self, he took delight
Luxurious in her sorrows, soft and new.
His passion, cruel grown, took on a hue   75
Fierce and sanguineous as 'twas possible
In one whose brow had no dark veins to swell.
Fine was the mitigated fury, like
Apollo's presence when in act to strike
The serpent—Ha, the serpent! certes, she   80
Was none. She burnt, she lov'd the tyranny,
And, all subdued, consented to the hour
When to the bridal he should lead his paramour.
Whispering in midnight silence, said the youth,
'Sure some sweet name thou hast, though, by my   85
    truth,
'I have not ask'd it, ever thinking thee
'Not mortal, but of heavenly progeny,
'As still I do. Hast any mortal name,
'Fit appellation for this dazzling frame?
'Or friends or kinsfolk on the citied earth,   90
'To share our marriage feast and nuptial mirth?'
'I have no friends,' said Lamia, 'no, not one;
'My presence in wide Corinth hardly known:
'My parents' bones are in their dusty urns
'Sepulchred, where no kindled incense burns,   95
'Seeing all their luckless race are dead, save me,
'And I neglect the holy rite for thee.
'Even as you list invite your many guests;
'But if, as now it seems, your vision rests
'With any pleasure on me, do not bid   100

'Old Apollonius—from him keep me hid.'
Lycius, perplex'd at words so blind and blank,
Made close inquiry; from whose touch she shrank,
Feigning a sleep; and he to the dull shade
Of deep sleep in a moment was betray'd.   105

    It was the custom then to bring away
The bride from home at blushing shut of day,
Veil'd, in a chariot, heralded along
By strewn flowers, torches, and a marriage song,
With other pageants: but this fair unknown   110
Had not a friend. So being left alone,
(Lycius was gone to summon all his kin)
And knowing surely she could never win
His foolish heart from its mad pompousness,
She set herself, high-thoughted, how to dress   115
The misery in fit magnificence.
She did so, but 'tis doubtful how and whence
Came, and who were her subtle servitors.
About the halls, and to and from the doors,
There was a noise of wings, till in short space   120
The glowing banquet-room shone with wide-arched
    grace.
A haunting music, sole perhaps and lone
Supportress of the faery-roof, made moan
Throughout, as fearful the whole charm might fade.
Fresh carved cedar, mimicking a glade   125
Of palm and plantain, met from either side,
High in the midst, in honour of the bride:
Two palms and then two plantains, and so on,
From either side their stems branch'd one to one
All down the aisled place; and beneath all   130
There ran a stream of lamps straight on from wall to
    wall.
So canopied, lay an untasted feast
Teeming with odours. Lamia, regal drest,

Silently paced about, and as she went,
In pale contented sort of discontent,   135
Mission'd her viewless servants to enrich
The fretted splendour of each nook and niche.
Between the tree-stems, marbled plain at first,
Came jasper pannels; then, anon, there burst
Forth creeping imagery of slighter trees,   140
And with the larger wove in small intricacies.
Approving all, she faded at self-will,
And shut the chamber up, close, hush'd and still,
Complete and ready for the revels rude,
When dreadful guests would come to spoil her soli-
    tude.   145

    The day appear'd, and all the gossip rout.
O senseless Lycius! Madman! wherefore flout
The silent-blessing fate, warm cloister'd hours,
And show to common eyes these secret bowers?
The herd approach'd; each guest, with busy brain,   150
Arriving at the portal, gaz'd amain,
And enter'd marveling: for they knew the street,
Remember'd it from childhood all complete
Without a gap, yet ne'er before had seen
That royal porch, that high-built fair demesne;   155
So in they hurried all, maz'd, curious and keen:
Save one, who look'd thereon with eye severe,
And with calm-planted steps walk'd in austere;
'Twas Apollonius: something too he laugh'd,
As though some knotty problem, that had daft   160
His patient thought, had now begun to thaw,
And solve and melt:—'twas just as he foresaw.

    He met within the murmurous vestibule
His young disciple. "Tis no common rule,
'Lycius,' said he, 'for uninvited guest   165
'To force himself upon you, and infest

34

'With an unbidden presence the bright throng
'Of younger friends; yet must I do this wrong,
'And you forgive me.' Lycius blush'd, and led
The old man through the inner doors broad-spread; 170
With reconciling words and courteous mien
Turning into sweet milk the sophist's spleen.

Of wealthy lustre was the banquet-room,
Fill'd with pervading brilliance and perfume:
Before each lucid pannel fuming stood   175
A censer fed with myrrh and spiced wood,
Each by a sacred tripod held aloft,
Whose slender feet wide-swerv'd upon the soft
Wool-woofed carpets: fifty wreaths of smoke
From fifty censers their light voyage took   180
To the high roof, still mimick'd as they rose
Along the mirror'd walls by twin-clouds odorous.
Twelve sphered tables, by silk seats insphered,
High as the level of a man's breast rear'd
On libbard's paws, upheld the heavy gold   185
Of cups and goblets, and the store thrice told
Of Ceres' horn, and, in huge vessels, wine
Come from the gloomy tun with merry shine.
Thus loaded with a feast the tables stood,
Each shrining in the midst the image of a God.   190

When in an antichamber every guest
Had felt the cold full sponge to pleasure press'd,
By minist'ring slaves, upon his hands and feet,
And fragrant oils with ceremony meet
Pour'd on his hair, they all mov'd to the feast   195
In white robes, and themselves in order placed
Around the silken couches, wondering
Whence all this mighty cost and blaze of wealth
    could spring.

Soft went the music the soft air along,
While fluent Greek a vowel'd undersong   200
Kept up among the guests, discoursing low
At first, for scarcely was the wine at flow;
But when the happy vintage touch'd their brains,
Louder they talk, and louder come the strains
Of powerful instruments:—the gorgeous dyes,   205
The space, the splendour of the draperies,
The roof of awful richness, nectarous cheer,
Beautiful slaves, and Lamia's self, appear,
Now, when the wine has done its rosy deed,
And every soul from human trammels freed,   210
No more so strange; for merry wine, sweet wine,
Will make Elysian shades not too fair, too divine.
Soon was God Bacchus at meridian height;
Flush'd were their cheeks, and bright eyes double
        bright:
Garlands of every green, and every scent   215
From vales deflower'd, or forest-trees branch-rent,
In baskets of bright osier'd gold were brought
High as the handles heap'd, to suit the thought
Of every guest; that each, as he did please,
Might fancy-fit his brows, silk-pillow'd at his ease. 220

    What wreath for Lamia? What for Lycius?
What for the sage, old Apollonius?
Upon her aching forehead be there hung
The leaves of willow and of adder's tongue;
And for the youth, quick, let us strip for him   225
The thyrsus, that his watching eyes may swim
Into forgetfulness; and, for the sage,
Let spear-grass and the spiteful thistle wage
War on his temples. Do not all charms fly
At the mere touch of cold philosophy?   230
There was an awful rainbow once in heaven:
We know her woof, her texture; she is given

In the dull catalogue of common things.
Philosophy will clip an Angel's wings,
Conquer all mysteries by rule and line,   235
Empty the haunted air, and gnomed mine—
Unweave a rainbow, as it erewhile made
The tender-person'd Lamia melt into a shade.

By her glad Lycius sitting, in chief place,
Scarce saw in all the room another face,   240
Till, checking his love trance, a cup he took
Full brimm'd, and opposite sent forth a look
'Cross the broad table, to beseech a glance
From his old teacher's wrinkled countenance,
And pledge him. The bald-head philosopher   245
Had fix'd his eye, without a twinkle or stir
Full on the alarmed beauty of the bride,
Brow-beating her fair form, and troubling her sweet
        pride.
Lycius then press'd her hand, with devout touch,
As pale it lay upon the rosy couch: 250
'Twas icy, and the cold ran through his veins;
Then sudden it grew hot, and all the pains
Of an unnatural heat shot to his heart.
'Lamia, what means this? Wherefore dost thou start?
'Know'st thou that man?' Poor Lamia answer'd not.   255
He gaz'd into her eyes, and not a jot
Own'd they the lovelorn piteous appeal:
More, more he gaz'd: his human senses reel:
Some hungry spell that loveliness absorbs;
There was no recognition in those orbs.   260
'Lamia!' he cried—and no soft-toned reply.
The many heard, and the loud revelry
Grew hush; the stately music no more breathes;
The myrtle sicken'd in a thousand wreaths.
By faint degrees, voice, lute, and pleasure ceased;   265
A deadly silence step by step increased,

Until it seem'd a horrid presence there,
And not a man but felt the terror in his hair.
'Lamia!' he shriek'd; and nothing but the shriek
With its sad echo did the silence break.   270
'Begone, foul dream!' he cried, gazing again
In the bride's face, where now no azure vein
Wander'd on fair-spaced temples; no soft bloom
Misted the cheek; no passion to illume
The deep-recessed vision:—all was blight;   275
Lamia, no longer fair, there sat a deadly white.
'Shut, shut those juggling eyes, thou ruthless man!
'Turn them aside, wretch! or the righteous ban
'Of all the Gods, whose dreadful images
'Here represent their shadowy presences,   280
'May pierce them on the sudden with the thorn
'Of painful blindness; leaving thee forlorn,
'In trembling dotage to the feeblest fright
'Of conscience, for their long offended might,
'For all thine impious proud-heart sophistries,   285
'Unlawful magic, and enticing lies.
'Corinthians! look upon that gray-beard wretch!
'Mark how, possess'd, his lashless eyelids stretch
'Around his demon eyes! Corinthians, see!
'My sweet bride withers at their potency.'   290
'Fool!' said the sophist, in an under-tone
Gruff with contempt; which a death-nighing moan
From Lycius answer'd, as heart-struck and lost,
He sank supine beside the aching ghost.
'Fool! Fool!' repeated he, while his eyes still   295
Relented not, nor mov'd; 'from every ill
'Of life have I preserv'd thee to this day,
'And shall I see thee made a serpent's prey?'
Then Lamia breath'd death breath; the sophist's
     eye,
Like a sharp spear, went through her utterly,   300
Keen, cruel, perceant, stinging: she, as well

As her weak hand could any meaning tell,
Motion'd him to be silent; vainly so,
He look'd and look'd again a level—No!
'A Serpent!' echoed he; no sooner said,   305
Than with a frightful scream she vanished:
And Lycius' arms were empty of delight,
As were his limbs of life, from that same night.
On the high couch he lay!—his friends came round—
Supported him—no pulse, or breath they found,   310
And, in its marriage robe, the heavy body wound.*

* 'Philostratus, in his fourth book *de Vita Apollonii*, hath a memorable instance in this kind, which I may not omit, of one Menippus Lycius, a young man twenty-five years of age, that going betwixt Cenchreas and Corinth, met such a phantasm in the habit of a fair gentlewoman, which taking him by the hand, carried him home to her house, in the suburbs of Corinth, and told him she was a Phœnician by birth, and if he would tarry with her, he should hear her sing and play, and drink such wine as never any drank, and no man should molest him; but she, being fair and lovely, would live and die with him, that was fair and lovely to behold. The young man, a philosopher, otherwise staid and discreet, able to moderate his passions, though not this of love, tarried with her a while to his great content, and at last married her, to whose wedding, amongst other guests, came Apollonius; who, by some probable conjectures, found her out to be a serpent, a lamia: and that all her furniture was, like Tantalus' gold, described by Homer, no substance but mere illusions. When she saw herself descried, she wept, and desired Apollonius to be silent, but he would not be moved, and thereupon she, plate, house, and all that was in it, vanished in an instant: many thousands took notice of this fact, for it was done in the midst of Greece.'

Burton's 'Anatomy of Melancholy.'
Part 3. Sect. 2. Memb. 1. Subs. 1

39

ISABELLA

OR,

THE POT OF BASIL

I

Fair Isabel, poor simple Isabel!
   Lorenzo, a young palmer in Love's eye!
They could not in the self-same mansion dwell
   Without some stir of heart, some malady;
They could not sit at meals but feel how well   5
   It soothed each to be the other by;
They could not, sure, beneath the same roof sleep
But to each other dream, and nightly weep.

II

With every morn their love grew tenderer,
   With every eve deeper and tenderer still;   10
He might not in house, field, or garden stir,
   But her full shape would all his seeing fill;
And his continual voice was pleasanter
   To her, than noise of trees or hidden rill;
Her lute-string gave an echo of his name,   15
She spoilt her half-done broidery with the same.

III

He knew whose gentle hand was at the latch,
   Before the door had given her to his eyes;
And from her chamber-window he would catch
   Her beauty farther than the falcon spies;   20

And constant as her vespers would he watch,
    Because her face was turn'd to the same skies;
And with sick longing all the night outwear,
To hear her morning-step upon the stair.

IV

A whole long month of May in this sad plight   25
    Made their cheeks paler by the break of June:
'To-morrow will I bow to my delight,
    'To-morrow will I ask my lady's boon.'—
'O may I never see another night,
    'Lorenzo, if thy lips breathe not love's tune.'—   30
So spake they to their pillows; but, alas,
Honeyless days and days did he let pass;

V

Until sweet Isabella's untouch'd cheek
    Fell sick within the rose's just domain,
Fell thin as a young mother's, who doth seek   35
    By every lull to cool her infant's pain:
'How ill she is,' said he, 'I may not speak,
    'And yet I will, and tell my love all plain:
'If looks speak love-laws, I will drink her tears,
    'And at the least 'twill startle off her cares.'   40

VI

So said he one fair morning, and all day
    His heart beat awfully against his side;
And to his heart he inwardly did pray
    For power to speak; but still the ruddy tide
Stifled his voice, and puls'd resolve away—   45
    Fever'd his high conceit of such a bride,
Yet brought him to the meekness of a child:
Alas! when passion is both meek and wild!

41

VII

So once more he had wak'd and anguished
   A dreary night of love and misery,   50
If Isabel's quick eye had not been wed
   To every symbol on his forehead high;
She saw it waxing very pale and dead,
   And straight all flush'd; so, lisped tenderly,
'Lorenzo!'—here she ceas'd her timid quest,   55
But in her tone and look he read the rest.

VIII

'O Isabella, I can half perceive
   'That I may speak my grief into thine ear;
'If thou didst ever any thing believe,
   'Believe how I love thee, believe how near   60
'My soul is to its doom: I would not grieve
   'Thy hand by unwelcome pressing, would not fear
'Thine eyes by gazing; but I cannot live
'Another night, and not my passion shrive.

IX

'Love! thou art leading me from wintry cold,   65
   'Lady! thou leadest me to summer clime,
'And I must taste the blossoms that unfold
   'In its ripe warmth this gracious morning time.'
So said, his erewhile timid lips grew bold,
   And poesied with hers in dewy rhyme: 70
Great bliss was with them, and great happiness
Grew, like a lusty flower in June's caress.

X

Parting they seem'd to tread upon the air,
   Twin roses by the zephyr blown apart
Only to meet again more close, and share   75
   The inward fragrance of each other's heart.

She, to her chamber gone, a ditty fair
  Sang, of delicious love and honey'd dart;
He with light steps went up a western hill,
And bade the sun farewell, and joy'd his fill.   80

XI

All close they met again, before the dusk
  Had taken from the stars its pleasant veil,
All close they met, all eves, before the dusk
  Had taken from the stars its pleasant veil,
Close in a bower of hyacinth and musk,   85
  Unknown of any, free from whispering tale.
Ah! better had it been for ever so,
Than idle ears should pleasure in their woe.

XII

Were they unhappy then?—It cannot be—
  Too many tears for lovers have been shed,   90
Too many sighs give we to them in fee,
  Too much of pity after they are dead,
Too many doleful stories do we see,
  Whose matter in bright gold were best be read;
Except in such a page where Theseus' spouse   95
Over the pathless waves towards him bows.

XIII

But, for the general award of love,
  The little sweet doth kill much bitterness;
Though Dido silent is in under-grove,
  And Isabella's was a great distress,   100
Though young Lorenzo in warm Indian clove
  Was not embalm'd, this truth is not the less—
Even bees, the little almsmen of spring-bowers,
Know there is richest juice in poison-flowers.

XIV

With her two brothers this fair lady dwelt,   105
  Enriched from ancestral merchandize,
And for them many a weary hand did swelt
  In torched mines and noisy factories,
And many once proud-quiver'd loins did melt
  In blood from stinging whip;—with hollow eyes   110
Many all day in dazzling river stood,
To take the rich-ored driftings of the flood.

XV

For them the Ceylon diver held his breath,
  And went all naked to the hungry shark;
For them his ears gush'd blood; for them in death   115
  The seal on the cold ice with piteous bark
Lay full of darts; for them alone did seethe
  A thousand men in troubles wide and dark:
Half-ignorant, they turn'd an easy wheel,
That set sharp racks at work, to pinch and peel.   120

XVI

Why were they proud? Because their marble founts
  Gush'd with more pride than do a wretch's tears?—
Why were they proud? Because fair orange-mounts
  Were of more soft ascent than lazar stairs?—
Why were they proud? Because red-lin'd accounts   125
  Were richer than the songs of Grecian years?—
Why were they proud? again we ask aloud,
Why in the name of Glory were they proud?

XVII

Yet were these Florentines as self-retired
  In hungry pride and gainful cowardice,   130
As two close Hebrews in that land inspired,
  Paled in and vineyarded from beggar-spies

The hawks of ship-mast forests—the untired
   And pannier'd mules for ducats and old lies—
Quick cat's-paws on the generous stray-away,—   135
Great wits in Spanish, Tuscan, and Malay.

XVIII

How was it these same ledger-men could spy
   Fair Isabella in her downy nest?
How could they find out in Lorenzo's eye
   A straying from his toil? Hot Egypt's pest   140
Into their vision covetous and sly!
   How could these money-bags see east and west?—
Yet so they did—and every dealer fair
Must see behind, as doth the hunted hare.

XIX

O eloquent and famed Boccaccio!   145
   Of thee we now should ask forgiving boon;
And of thy spicy myrtles as they blow,
   And of thy roses amorous of the moon,
And of thy lilies, that do paler grow
   Now they can no more hear thy ghittern's tune,   150
For venturing syllables that ill beseem
The quiet glooms of such a piteous theme.

XX

Grant thou a pardon here, and then the tale
   Shall move on soberly, as it is meet;
There is no other crime, no mad assail   155
   To make old prose in modern rhyme more sweet:
But it is done—succeed the verse or fail—
   To honour thee, and thy gone spirit greet;
To stead thee as a verse in English tongue,
An echo of thee in the north-wind sung.   160

XXI

These brethren having found by many signs
   What love Lorenzo for their sister had,
And how she lov'd him too, each unconfines
   His bitter thoughts to other, well nigh mad
That he, the servant of their trade designs,   165
   Should in their sister's love be blithe and glad,
When 'twas their plan to coax her by degrees
To some high noble and his olive-trees.

XXII

And many a jealous conference had they,
   And many times they bit their lips alone,   170
Before they fix'd upon a surest way
   To make the youngster for his crime atone;
And at the last, these men of cruel clay
   Cut Mercy with a sharp knife to the bone;
For they resolved in some forest dim   175
To kill Lorenzo, and there bury him.

XXIII

So on a pleasant morning, as he leant
   Into the sun-rise, o'er the balustrade
Of the garden-terrace, towards him they bent
   Their footing through the dews; and to him said,   180
'You seem there in the quiet of content,
   'Lorenzo, and we are most loth to invade
'Calm speculation; but if you are wise,
'Bestride your steed while cold is in the skies.

XXIV

'To-day we purpose, ay, this hour we mount   185
   'To spur three leagues towards the Apennine;
'Come down, we pray thee, ere the hot sun count
   'His dewy rosary on the eglantine.'

Lorenzo, courteously as he was wont,
    Bow'd a fair greeting to these serpents' whine;   190
And went in haste, to get in readiness,
With belt, and spur, and bracing huntsman's dress.

XXV

And as he to the court-yard pass'd along,
    Each third step did he pause, and listen'd oft
If he could hear his lady's matin-song,   195
    Or the light whisper of her footstep soft;
And as he thus over his passion hung,
    He heard a laugh full musical aloft;
When, looking up, he saw her features bright
Smile through an in-door lattice, all delight.   200

XXVI

'Love, Isabel!' said he, 'I was in pain
    'Lest I should miss to bid thee a good morrow
'Ah! what if I should lose thee, when so fain
    'I am to stifle all the heavy sorrow
'Of a poor three hours' absence? but we'll gain   205
    'Out of the amorous dark what day doth borrow.
'Good bye! I'll soon be back.'—'Good bye!' said
    she:—
And as he went she chanted merrily.

XXVII

So the two brothers and their murder'd man
    Rode past fair Florence, to where Arno's stream   210
Gurgles through straiten'd banks, and still doth fan
    Itself with dancing bulrush, and the bream
Keeps head against the freshets. Sick and wan
    The brothers' faces in the ford did seem,
Lorenzo's flush with love.—They pass'd the water   215
Into a forest quiet for the slaughter.

XXVIII

There was Lorenzo slain and buried in,
   There in that forest did his great love cease;
Ah! when a soul doth thus its freedom win,
   It aches in loneliness—is ill at peace   220
As the break-covert blood-hounds of such sin:
   They dipp'd their swords in the water, and did
     tease
Their horses homeward, with convulsed spur,
Each richer by his being a murderer.

XXIX

They told their sister how, with sudden speed,   225
   Lorenzo had ta'en ship for foreign lands,
Because of some great urgency and need
   In their affairs, requiring trusty hands.
Poor Girl! put on thy stifling widow's weed,
   And 'scape at once from Hope's accursed bands;   230
To-day thou wilt not see him, nor to-morrow,
And the next day will be a day of sorrow.

XXX

She weeps alone for pleasures not to be;
   Sorely she wept until the night came on,
And then, instead of love, O misery!   235
   She brooded o'er the luxury alone:
His image in the dusk she seem'd to see,
   And to the silence made a gentle moan,
Spreading her perfect arms upon the air,
And on her couch low murmuring 'Where?   240
   O where?'

XXXI

But Selfishness, Love's cousin, held not long
   Its fiery vigil in her single breast;
She fretted for the golden hour, and hung
   Upon the time with feverish unrest—

Not long—for soon into her heart a throng   245
   Of higher occupants, a richer zest,
Came tragic; passion not to be subdued,
And sorrow for her love in travels rude.

XXXII

In the mid days of autumn, on their eves,
   The breath of Winter comes from far away,   250
And the sick west continually bereaves
   Of some gold tinge, and plays a roundelay
Of death among the bushes and the leaves
   To make all bare before he dares to stray
From his north cavern. So sweet Isabel   255
By gradual decay from beauty fell,

XXXIII

Because Lorenzo came not. Oftentimes
   She ask'd her brothers, with an eye all pale,
Striving to be itself, what dungeon climes
   Could keep him off so long? They spake a tale   260
Time after time, to quiet her. Their crimes
   Came on them, like a smoke from Hinnom's vale;
And every night in dreams they groan'd aloud,
To see their sister in her snowy shroud.

XXXIV

And she had died in drowsy ignorance,   265
   But for a thing more deadly dark than all;
It came like a fierce potion, drunk by chance,
   Which saves a sick man from the feather'd pall
For some few gasping moments; like a lance,
   Waking an Indian from his cloudy hall   270
With cruel pierce, and bringing him again
Sense of the gnawing fire at heart and brain.

49

XXXV

It was a vision.—In the drowsy gloom,
   The dull of midnight, at her couch's foot
Lorenzo stood, and wept: the forest tomb   275
   Had marr'd his glossy hair which once could shoot
Lustre into the sun, and put cold doom
   Upon his lips, and taken the soft lute
From his lorn voice, and past his loamed ears
Had made a miry channel for his tears.   280

XXXVI

Strange sound it was, when the pale shadow spake;
   For there was striving, in its piteous tongue,
To speak as when on earth it was awake,
   And Isabella on its music hung:
Languor there was in it, and tremulous shake,   285
   As in a palsied Druid's harp unstrung;
And through it moan'd a ghostly under-song,
Like hoarse night-gusts sepulchral briars among.

XXXVII

Its eyes, though wild, were still all dewy bright
   With love, and kept all phantom fear aloof   290
From the poor girl by magic of their light,
   The while it did unthread the horrid woof
Of the late darken'd time,—the murderous spite
   Of pride and avarice,—the dark pine roof
In the forest,—and the sodden turfed dell,   295
Where, without any word, from stabs he fell.

XXXVIII

Saying moreover, 'Isabel, my sweet!
   'Red whortle-berries droop above my head,
'And a large flint-stone weighs upon my feet;
   'Around me beeches and high chestnuts shed   300

'Their leaves and prickly nuts; a sheep-fold bleat
  'Comes from beyond the river to my bed:
'Go, shed one tear upon my heather-bloom,
'And it shall comfort me within the tomb.

XXXIX

'I am a shadow now, alas! alas!   305
  'Upon the skirts of human-nature dwelling
'Alone: I chant alone the holy mass,
  'While little sounds of life are round me knelling,
'And glossy bees at noon do fieldward pass,
  'And many a chapel bell the hour is telling,   310
'Paining me through: those sounds grow strange
      to me,
'And thou art distant in Humanity.

XL

'I know what was, I feel full well what is,
  'And I should rage, if spirits could go mad;
'Though I forget the taste of earthly bliss,   315
  'That paleness warms my grave, as though I had
'A Seraph chosen from the bright abyss
  'To be my spouse: thy paleness makes me glad;
'Thy beauty grows upon me, and I feel
'A greater love through all my essence steal.'   320

XLI

The Spirit mourn'd 'Adieu!'—dissolv'd, and left
  The atom darkness in a slow turmoil;
As when of healthful midnight sleep bereft,
  Thinking on rugged hours and fruitless toil,
We put our eyes into a pillowy cleft,   325
  And see the spangly gloom froth up and boil:
It made sad Isabella's eyelids ache,
And in the dawn she started up awake;

51

XLII

'Ha! ha!' said she, 'I knew not this hard life,
  'I thought the worst was simple misery;   330
'I thought some Fate with pleasure or with strife
  'Portion'd us—happy days, or else to die;
'But there is crime—a brother's bloody knife!
  'Sweet Spirit, thou hast school'd my infancy:
'I'll visit thee for this, and kiss thine eyes,   335
'And greet thee morn and even in the skies.'

XLIII

When the full morning came, she had devised
  How she might secret to the forest hie;
How she might find the clay, so dearly prized,
  And sing to it one latest lullaby;   340
How her short absence might be unsurmised,
  While she the inmost of the dream would try.
Resolv'd, she took with her an aged nurse,
And went into that dismal forest-hearse.

XLIV

See, as they creep along the river side,   345
  How she doth whisper to that aged Dame,
And, after looking round the champaign wide,
  Shows her a knife.—'What feverous hectic flame
'Burns in thee, child?—What good can thee betide,
  'That thou should'st smile again?'—The evening 350
    came,
And they had found Lorenzo's earthy bed;
The flint was there, the berries at his head.

XLV

Who hath not loiter'd in a green church-yard,
  And let his spirit, like a demon-mole,
Work through the clayey soil and gravel hard,   355
  To see scull, coffin'd bones, and funeral stole;

Pitying each form that hungry Death hath marr'd,
    And filling it once more with human soul?
Ah! this is holiday to what was felt
When Isabella by Lorenzo knelt.   360

XLVI

She gaz'd into the fresh-thrown mould, as though
    One glance did fully all its secrets tell;
Clearly she saw, as other eyes would know
    Pale limbs at bottom of a crystal well;
Upon the murderous spot she seem'd to grow,   365
    Like to a native lily of the dell:
Then with her knife, all sudden, she began
To dig more fervently than misers can.

XLVII

Soon she turn'd up a soiled glove, whereon
    Her silk had play'd in purple phantasies,   370
She kiss'd it with a lip more chill than stone,
    And put it in her bosom, where it dries
And freezes utterly unto the bone
    Those dainties made to still an infant's cries:
Then 'gan she work again; nor stay'd her care,   375
But to throw back at times her veiling hair.

XLVIII

That old nurse stood beside her wondering,
    Until her heart felt pity to the core
At sight of such a dismal labouring,
    And so she kneeled, with her locks all hoar,   380
And put her lean hands to the horrid thing:
    Three hours they labour'd at this travail sore;
At last they felt the kernel of the grave,
And Isabella did not stamp and rave.

XLIX

Ah! wherefore all this wormy circumstance?   385
 Why linger at the yawning tomb so long?
O for the gentleness of old Romance,
 The simple plaining of a minstrel's song!
Fair reader, at the old tale take a glance,
 For here, in truth, it doth not well belong   390
To speak:—O turn thee to the very tale,
And taste the music of that vision pale.

L

With duller steel than the Perséan sword
 They cut away no formless monster's head,
But one, whose gentleness did well accord   395
 With death, as life. The ancient harps have said,
Love never dies, but lives, immortal Lord:
 If Love impersonate was ever dead,
Pale Isabella kiss'd it, and low moan'd.
'Twas love; cold,—dead indeed, but not dethroned. 400

LI

In anxious secrecy they took it home,
 And then the prize was all for Isabel:
She calm'd its wild hair with a golden comb,
 And all around each eye's sepulchral cell
Pointed each fringed lash; the smeared loam   405
 With tears, as chilly as a dripping well,
She drench'd away:—and still she comb'd, and kept
Sighing all day—and still she kiss'd, and wept.

LII

Then in a silken scarf,—sweet with the dews
 Of precious flowers pluck'd in Araby,   410
And divine liquids come with odorous ooze
 Through the cold serpent-pipe refreshfully,—

She wrapp'd it up; and for its tomb did choose
   A garden-pot, wherein she laid it by,
And cover'd it with mould, and o'er it set   415
Sweet Basil, which her tears kept ever wet.

LIII

And she forgot the stars, the moon, and sun,
   And she forgot the blue above the trees,
And she forgot the dells where waters run,
   And she forgot the chilly autumn breeze;   420
She had no knowledge when the day was done,
   And the new morn she saw not: but in peace
Hung over her sweet Basil evermore,
And moisten'd it with tears unto the core.

LIV

And so she ever fed it with thin tears,   425
   Whence thick, and green, and beautiful it grew,
So that it smelt more balmy than its peers
   Of Basil-tufts in Florence; for it drew
Nurture besides, and life, from human fears,
   From the fast mouldering head there shut from
      view: 430
So that the jewel, safely casketed,
Came forth, and in perfumed leafits spread.

LV

O Melancholy, linger here awhile!
   O Music, Music, breathe despondingly!
O Echo, Echo, from some sombre isle,   435
   Unknown, Lethean, sigh to us—O sigh!
Spirits in grief, lift up your heads, and smile;
   Lift up your heads, sweet Spirits, heavily,
And make a pale light in your cypress glooms,
Tinting with silver wan your marble tombs.   440

LVI

Moan hither, all ye syllables of woe,
　　From the deep throat of sad Melpomene!
Through bronzed lyre in tragic order go,
　　And touch the strings into a mystery;
Sound mournfully upon the winds and low;　　　445
　　For simple Isabel is soon to be
Among the dead: She withers, like a palm
Cut by an Indian for its juicy balm.

LVII

O leave the palm to wither by itself;
　　Let not quick Winter chill its dying hour!—　　450
It may not be—those Baälites of pelf,
　　Her brethren, noted the continual shower
From her dead eyes; and many a curious elf,
　　Among her kindred, wonder'd that such dower
Of youth and beauty should be thrown aside　　　455
By one mark'd out to be a Noble's bride.

LVIII

And, furthermore, her brethren wonder'd much
　　Why she sat drooping by the Basil green,
And why it flourish'd, as by magic touch;
　　Greatly they wonder'd what the thing might mean:　460
They could not surely give belief, that such
　　A very nothing would have power to wean
Her from her own fair youth, and pleasures gay,
And even remembrance of her love's delay.

LIX

Therefore they watch'd a time when they might sift　465
　　This hidden whim; and long they watch'd in vain;
For seldom did she go to chapel-shrift,
　　And seldom felt she any hunger-pain;

And when she left, she hurried back, as swift
    As bird on wing to breast its eggs again;   470
And, patient as a hen-bird, sat her there
Beside her Basil, weeping through her hair.

LX

Yet they contriv'd to steal the Basil-pot,
    And to examine it in secret place:
The thing was vile with green and livid spot,   475
    And yet they knew it was Lorenzo's face:
The guerdon of their murder they had got,
    And so left Florence in a moment's space,
Never to turn again.—Away they went,
With blood upon their heads, to banishment.   480

LXI

O Melancholy, turn thine eyes away!
    O Music, Music, breathe despondingly!
O Echo, Echo, on some other day,
    From isles Lethean, sigh to us—O sigh!
Spirits of grief, sing not your 'Well-a-way!'   485
    For Isabel, sweet Isabel, will die;
Will die a death too lone and incomplete,
Now they have ta'en away her Basil sweet.

LXII

Piteous she look'd on dead and senseless things,
    Asking for her lost Basil amorously;   490
And with melodious chuckle in the strings
    Of her lorn voice, she oftentimes would cry
After the Pilgrim in his wanderings,
    To ask him where her Basil was; and why
'Twas hid from her: 'For cruel 'tis,' said she,   495
'To steal my Basil-pot away from me.'

LXIII

And so she pined, and so she died forlorn,
   Imploring for her Basil to the last.
No heart was there in Florence but did mourn
   In pity of her love, so overcast.   500
And a sad ditty of this story born
   From mouth to mouth through all the country
      pass'd:
Still is the burthen sung—'O cruelty,
'To steal my Basil-pot away from me!'

THE EVE OF ST. AGNES

I

St. Agnes' Eve—Ah, bitter chill it was!
The owl, for all his feathers, was a-cold;
The hare limp'd trembling through the frozen
    grass,
And silent was the flock in woolly fold:
Numb were the Beadsman's fingers, while he told   5
His rosary, and while his frosted breath,
Like pious incense from a censer old,
Seem'd taking flight for heaven, without a death,
Past the sweet Virgin's picture, while his prayer he
    saith.

II

His prayer he saith, this patient, holy man;   10
Then takes his lamp, and riseth from his knees,
And back returneth, meagre, barefoot, wan,
Along the chapel aisle by slow degrees:
The sculptur'd dead, on each side, seem to freeze,
Emprison'd in black, purgatorial rails: 15
Knights, ladies, praying in dumb orat'ries,
He passeth by; and his weak spirit fails
To think how they may ache in icy hoods and mails.

III

Northward he turneth through a little door,
And scarce three steps, ere Music's golden tongue   20
Flatter'd to tears this aged man and poor;
But no—already had his deathbell rung;
The joys of all his life were said and sung:
His was harsh penance on St. Agnes' Eve:
Another way he went, and soon among   25
Rough ashes sat he for his soul's reprieve,
And all night kept awake, for sinners' sake to grieve.

IV

That ancient Beadsman heard the prelude soft;
And so it chanc'd, for many a door was wide,
From hurry to and fro. Soon, up aloft,   30
The silver, snarling trumpets 'gan to chide:
The level chambers, ready with their pride,
Were glowing to receive a thousand guests:
The carved angels, ever eager-eyed,
  Star'd, where upon their heads the cornice rests, 35
With hair blown back, and wings put cross-wise on
    their breasts.

V

At length burst in the argent revelry,
With plume, tiara, and all rich array,
Numerous as shadows haunting fairily
The brain, new stuff'd, in youth, with triumphs 40
  gay
Of old romance. These let us wish away,
And turn, sole-thoughted, to one Lady there,
Whose heart had brooded, all that wintry day,
  On love, and wing'd St. Agnes' saintly care,
As she had heard old dames full many times declare. 45

VI

They told her how, upon St. Agnes' Eve,
Young virgins might have visions of delight,
And soft adorings from their loves receive
Upon the honey'd middle of the night,
If ceremonies due they did aright;   50
As, supperless to bed they must retire,
And couch supine their beauties, lily white;
  Nor look behind, nor sideways, but require
Of Heaven with upward eyes for all that they desire.

VII

Full of this whim was thoughtful Madeline: 55
The music, yearning like a God in pain,
She scarcely heard: her maiden eyes divine,
Fix'd on the floor, saw many a sweeping train
Pass by—she heeded not at all: in vain
Came many a tiptoe, amorous cavalier,   60
And back retir'd; not cool'd by high disdain,
But she saw not: her heart was otherwhere:
She sigh'd for Agnes' dreams, the sweetest of the
       year.

VIII

She danc'd along with vague, regardless eyes,
Anxious her lips, her breathing quick and short: 65
The hallow'd hour was near at hand: she sighs
Amid the timbrels, and the throng'd resort
Of whisperers in anger, or in sport;
'Mid looks of love, defiance, hate, and scorn,
Hoodwink'd with faery fancy; all amort,   70
Save to St. Agnes and her lambs unshorn,
And all the bliss to be before to-morrow morn.

IX

So, purposing each moment to retire,
She linger'd still. Meantime, across the moors,
Had come young Porphyro, with heart on fire   75
For Madeline. Beside the portal doors,
Buttress'd from moonlight, stands he, and implores
All saints to give him sight of Madeline,
But for one moment in the tedious hours,
That he might gaze and worship all unseen;   80
Perchance speak, kneel, touch, kiss—in sooth such
       things have been.

X

He ventures in: let no buzz'd whisper tell:
All eyes be muffled, or a hundred swords
Will storm his heart, Love's fev'rous citadel:
For him, those chambers held barbarian hordes,   85
Hyena foemen, and hot-blooded lords,
Whose very dogs would execrations howl
Against his lineage: not one breast affords
Him any mercy, in that mansion foul,
Save one old beldame, weak in body and in soul.   90

XI

Ah, happy chance! the aged creature came,
Shuffling along with ivory-headed wand,
To where he stood, hid from the torch's flame,
Behind a broad hall-pillar, far beyond
The sound of merriment and chorus bland: 95
He startled her; but soon she knew his face,
And grasp'd his fingers in her palsied hand,
Saying, 'Mercy, Porphyro! hie thee from this place;
'They are all here to-night, the whole blood-thirsty
    race!

XII

'Get hence! get hence! there's dwarfish Hildebrand;   100
'He had a fever late, and in the fit
'He cursed thee and thine, both house and land:
'Then there's that old Lord Maurice, not a whit
'More tame for his gray hairs—Alas me! flit!
'Flit like a ghost away.'—'Ah, Gossip dear,   105
'We're safe enough; here in this arm-chair sit,
'And tell me how'—'Good Saints! not here, not
    here;
'Follow me, child, or else these stones will be thy bier.'

XIII

He follow'd through a lowly arched way,
Brushing the cobwebs with his lofty plume,   110
And as she mutter'd 'Well-a—well-a-day!'
He found him in a little moonlight room,
Pale, lattic'd, chill, and silent as a tomb.
'Now tell me where is Madeline,' said he,
'O tell me, Angela, by the holy loom   115
'Which none but secret sisterhood may see,
'When they St. Agnes' wool are weaving piously.'

XIV

'St. Agnes! Ah! it is St. Agnes' Eve—
'Yet men will murder upon holy days:
'Thou must hold water in a witch's sieve,   120
'And be liege-lord of all the Elves and Fays,
'To venture so: it fills me with amaze
'To see thee, Porphyro!—St. Agnes' Eve!
'God's help! my lady fair the conjuror plays
'This very night: good angels her deceive!   125
'But let me laugh awhile, I've mickle time to grieve.'

XV

Feebly she laugheth in the languid moon,
While Porphyro upon her face doth look,
Like puzzled urchin on an aged crone
Who keepeth clos'd a wond'rous riddle-book,   130
As spectacled she sits in chimney nook.
But soon his eyes grew brilliant, when she told
His lady's purpose; and he scarce could brook
Tears, at the thought of those enchantments cold
And Madeline asleep in lap of legends old.   135

XVI

Sudden a thought came like a full-blown rose,
Flushing his brow, and in his pained heart
Made purple riot: then doth he propose
A stratagem, that makes the beldame start:
'A cruel man and impious thou art: 140
'Sweet lady, let her pray, and sleep, and dream
'Alone with her good angels, far apart
'From wicked men like thee. Go, go!—I deem
'Thou canst not surely be the same that thou didst
    seem.'

XVII

'I will not harm her, by all saints I swear,'   145
Quoth Porphyro: 'O may I ne'er find grace
'When my weak voice shall whisper its last prayer,
'If one of her soft ringlets I displace,
'Or look with ruffian passion in her face:
'Good Angela, believe me by these tears;   150
'Or I will, even in a moment's space,
'Awake, with horrid shout, my foemen's ears,
'And beard them, though they be more fang'd than
    wolves and bears.'

XVIII

'Ah! why wilt thou affright a feeble soul?
'A poor, weak, palsy-stricken, churchyard thing,   155
'Whose passing-bell may ere the midnight toll;
'Whose prayers for thee, each morn and evening,
'Were never miss'd.'—Thus plaining, doth she
    bring
A gentler speech from burning Porphyro;
So woful, and of such deep sorrowing,   160
That Angela gives promise she will do
Whatever he shall wish, betide her weal or woe.

XIX

Which was, to lead him, in close secrecy,
Even to Madeline's chamber, and there hide
Him in a closet, of such privacy   165
That he might see her beauty unespied,
And win perhaps that night a peerless bride,
While legion'd fairies pac'd the coverlet,
And pale enchantment held her sleepy-eyed.
Never on such a night have lovers met,   170
Since Merlin paid his Demon all the monstrous debt.

XX

'It shall be as thou wishest,' said the Dame:
'All cates and dainties shall be stored there
'Quickly on this feast-night: by the tambour frame
'Her own lute thou wilt see: no time to spare,   175
'For I am slow and feeble, and scarce dare
'On such a catering trust my dizzy head.
'Wait here, my child, with patience; kneel in prayer
'The while: Ah! thou must needs the lady wed,
'Or may I never leave my grave among the dead.'   180

XXI

So saying, she hobbled off with busy fear.
The lover's endless minutes slowly pass'd;
The dame return'd, and whisper'd in his ear
To follow her; with aged eyes aghast
From fright of dim espial. Safe at last,   185
Through many a dusky gallery, they gain
The maiden's chamber, silken, hush'd, and chaste;
Where Porphyro took covert, pleas'd amain.
His poor guide hurried back with agues in her brain.

XXII

Her falt'ring hand upon the balustrade, 190
Old Angela was feeling for the stair,
When Madeline, St. Agnes' charmed maid,
Rose, like a mission'd spirit, unaware:
With silver taper's light, and pious care,
She turn'd, and down the aged gossip led 195
To a safe level matting. Now prepare,
Young Porphyro, for gazing on that bed;
She comes, she comes again, like ring-dove fray'd
and fled.

XXIII

Out went the taper as she hurried in;
Its little smoke, in pallid moonshine, died: 200
She clos'd the door, she panted, all akin
To spirits of the air, and visions wide:
No utter'd syllable, or, woe betide!
But to her heart, her heart was voluble,
Paining with eloquence her balmy side; 205
As though a tongueless nightingale should swell
Her throat in vain, and die, heart-stifled, in her dell.

XXIV

A casement high and triple-arch'd there was,
All garlanded with carven imag'ries
Of fruits, and flowers, and bunches of knot-grass, 210
And diamonded with panes of quaint device,
Innumerable of stains and splendid dyes,
As are the tiger-moth's deep-damask'd wings;
And in the midst, 'mong thousand heraldries,
And twilight saints, and dim emblazonings, 215
A shielded scutcheon blush'd with blood of queens
and kings.

XXV

Full on this casement shone the wintry moon,
And threw warm gules on Madeline's fair breast,
As down she knelt for heaven's grace and boon;
Rose-bloom fell on her hands, together prest,   220
And on her silver cross soft amethyst,
And on her hair a glory, like a saint:
She seem'd a splendid angel, newly drest,
Save wings, for heaven:—Porphyro grew faint:
She knelt, so pure a thing, so free from mortal taint.   225

XXVI

Anon his heart revives: her vespers done,
Of all its wreathed pearls her hair she frees;
Unclasps her warmed jewels one by one;
Loosens her fragrant boddice; by degrees
Her rich attire creeps rustling to her knees: 230
Half-hidden, like a mermaid in sea-weed,
Pensive awhile she dreams awake, and sees,
In fancy, fair St. Agnes in her bed,
But dares not look behind, or all the charm is fled.

XXVII

Soon, trembling in her soft and chilly nest,   235
In sort of wakeful swoon, perplex'd she lay,
Until the poppied warmth of sleep oppress'd
Her soothed limbs, and soul fatigued away;
Flown, like a thought, until the morrow-day;
Blissfully haven'd both from joy and pain;   240
Clasp'd like a missal where swart Paynims pray;
Blinded alike from sunshine and from rain,
As though a rose should shut, and be a bud again.

XXVIII

Stol'n to this paradise, and so entranced,
Porphyro gazed upon her empty dress,   245
And listen'd to her breathing, if it chanced
To wake into a slumberous tenderness;
Which when he heard, that minute did he bless,
And breath'd himself: then from the closet crept,
Noiseless as fear in a wide wilderness,   250
And over the hush'd carpet, silent, stept,
And 'tween the curtains peep'd, where, lo!—how fast
    she slept.

XXIX

Then by the bed-side, where the faded moon
Made a dim, silver twilight, soft he set
A table, and, half anguish'd, threw thereon   255
A cloth of woven crimson, gold, and jet:—
O for some drowsy Morphean amulet!
The boisterous, midnight, festive clarion,
The kettle-drum, and far-heard clarionet,
Affray his ears, though but in dying tone:—   260
The hall door shuts again, and all the noise is gone.

XXX

And still she slept an azure-lidded sleep,
In blanched linen, smooth, and lavender'd,
While he from forth the closet brought a heap
Of candied apple, quince, and plum, and gourd   265
With jellies soother than the creamy curd,
And lucent syrops, tinct with cinnamon;
Manna and dates, in argosy transferr'd
From Fez; and spiced dainties, every one,
From silken Samarcand to cedar'd Lebanon.   270

XXXI

These delicates he heap'd with glowing hand
On golden dishes and in baskets bright
Of wreathed silver: sumptuous they stand
In the retired quiet of the night,
Filling the chilly room with perfume light.—   275
'And now, my love, my seraph fair, awake!
'Thou art my heaven, and I thine eremite:
'Open thine eyes, for meek St. Agnes' sake,
'Or I shall drowse beside thee, so my soul doth ache.'

XXXII

Thus whispering, his warm, unnerved arm   280
Sank in her pillow. Shaded was her dream
By the dusk curtains:—'twas a midnight charm
Impossible to melt as iced stream:
The lustrous salvers in the moonlight gleam;
Broad golden fringe upon the carpet lies: 285
It seem'd he never, never could redeem
From such a stedfast spell his lady's eyes;
So mus'd awhile, entoil'd in woofed phantasies.

XXXIII

Awakening up, he took her hollow lute,—
Tumultuous,—and, in chords that tenderest be,   290
He play'd an ancient ditty, long since mute,
In Provence call'd 'La belle dame sans mercy:'
Close to her ear touching the melody;—
Wherewith disturb'd, she utter'd a soft moan:
He ceased—she panted quick—and suddenly   295
Her blue affrayed eyes wide open shone:
Upon his knees he sank, pale as smooth-sculptured
    stone.

XXXIV

Her eyes were open, but she still beheld,
Now wide awake, the vision of her sleep:
There was a painful change, that nigh expell'd   300
The blisses of her dream so pure and deep
At which fair Madeline began to weep,
And moan forth witless words with many a sigh;
While still her gaze on Porphyro would keep;
Who knelt, with joined hands and piteous eye,   305
Fearing to move or speak, she look'd so dreamingly.

XXXV

'Ah, Porphyro!' said she, 'but even now
'Thy voice was at sweet tremble in mine ear,
'Made tuneable with every sweetest vow;
'And those sad eyes were spiritual and clear: 310
'How chang'd thou art! how pallid, chill, and drear!
'Give me that voice again, my Porphyro,
'Those looks immortal, those complainings dear!
'Oh leave me not in this eternal woe,
'For if thou diest, my Love, I know not where to go.'   315

XXXVI

Beyond a mortal man impassion'd far
At these voluptuous accents, he arose,
Ethereal, flush'd, and like a throbbing star
Seen mid the sapphire heaven's deep repose
Into her dream he melted, as the rose   320
Blendeth its odour with the violet,—
Solution sweet: meantime the frost-wind blows
Like Love's alarum pattering the sharp sleet
Against the window-panes; St. Agnes' moon hath set.

XXXVII

'Tis dark: quick pattereth the flaw-blown sleet: 325
'This is no dream, my bride, my Madeline!'
'Tis dark: the iced gusts still rave and beat:
'No dream, alas! alas! and woe is mine!
'Porphyro will leave me here to fade and pine.—
'Cruel! what traitor could thee hither bring?   330
'I curse not, for my heart is lost in thine
'Though thou forsakest a deceived thing;—
'A dove forlorn and lost with sick unpruned wing.'

XXXVIII

'My Madeline! sweet dreamer! lovely bride!
'Say, may I be for aye thy vassal blest?   335
'Thy beauty's shield, heart-shap'd and vermeil dyed?
'Ah, silver shrine, here will I take my rest
'After so many hours of toil and quest,
'A famish'd pilgrim,—saved by miracle.
'Though I have found, I will not rob thy nest   340
'Saving of thy sweet self; if thou think'st well
'To trust, fair Madeline, to no rude infidel.'

XXXIX

'Hark! 'tis an elfin-storm from faery land,
'Of haggard seeming, but a boon indeed:
'Arise—arise! the morning is at hand;—
'The bloated wassaillers will never heed:—   345
'Let us away, my love, with happy speed;
'There are no ears to hear, or eyes to see,—
'Drown'd all in Rhenish and the sleepy mead:
'Awake! arise! my love, and fearless be,   350
'For o'er the southern moors I have a home for thee.'

XL

She hurried at his words, beset with fears,
For there were sleeping dragons all around,
At glaring watch, perhaps, with ready spears—
Down the wide stairs a darkling way they found.— 355
In all the house was heard no human sound.
A chain-droop'd lamp was flickering by each door;
The arras, rich with horseman, hawk, and hound,
Flutter'd in the besieging wind's uproar;
And the long carpets rose along the gusty floor.   360

XLI

They glide, like phantoms, into the wide hall;
Like phantoms, to the iron porch, they glide;
Where lay the Porter, in uneasy sprawl,
With a huge empty flaggon by his side:
The wakeful bloodhound rose, and shook his hide, 365
But his sagacious eye an inmate owns:
By one, and one, the bolts full easy slide:—
The chains lie silent on the footworn stones;—
The key turns, and the door upon its hinges groans.

XLII

And they are gone: ay, ages long ago   370
These lovers fled away into the storm.
That night the Baron dreamt of many a woe,
And all his warrior-guests, with shade and form
Of witch, and demon, and large coffin-worm,
Were long be-nightmar'd. Angela the old   375
Died palsy-twitch'd, with meagre face deform;
The Beadsman, after thousand aves told,
For aye unsought for slept among his ashes cold.

ODE TO A NIGHTINGALE

1

My heart aches, and a drowsy numbness pains
  My sense, as though of hemlock I had drunk,
Or emptied some dull opiate to the drains
  One minute past, and Lethe-wards had sunk:
'Tis not through envy of thy happy lot,   5
  But being too happy in thine happiness,—
    That thou, light-winged Dryad of the trees,
      In some melodious plot
  Of beechen green, and shadows numberless,
    Singest of summer in full-throated ease.   10

2

O, for a draught of vintage! that hath been
  Cool'd a long age in the deep-delved earth,
Tasting of Flora and the country green,
  Dance, and Provençal song, and sunburnt mirth!
O for a beaker full of the warm South,   15
  Full of the true, the blushful Hippocrene,
    With beaded bubbles winking at the brim,
      And purple-stained mouth;
  That I might drink, and leave the world unseen,
    And with thee fade away into the forest dim: 20

3

Fade far away, dissolve, and quite forget
  What thou among the leaves hast never known,
The weariness, the fever, and the fret
  Here, where men sit and hear each other groan;
Where palsy shakes a few, sad, last gray hairs,   25
  Where youth grows pale, and spectre-thin, and dies;

73

Where but to think is to be full of sorrow
    And leaden-eyed despairs,
Where Beauty cannot keep her lustrous eyes,
    Or new Love pine at them beyond to-morrow.   30

4

Away! away! for I will fly to thee,
    Not charioted by Bacchus and his pards,
But on the viewless wings of Poesy,
    Though the dull brain perplexes and retards:
Already with thee! tender is the night,   35
    And haply the Queen-Moon is on her throne,
        Cluster'd around by all her starry Fays;
            But here there is no light,
    Save what from heaven is with the breezes blown
        Through verdurous glooms and winding mossy
            ways.   40

5

I cannot see what flowers are at my feet,
    Nor what soft incense hangs upon the boughs,
But, in embalmed darkness, guess each sweet
    Wherewith the seasonable month endows
The grass, the thicket, and the fruit-tree wild;   45
    White hawthorn, and the pastoral eglantine;
        Fast fading violets cover'd up in leaves;
            And mid-May's eldest child,
    The coming musk-rose, full of dewy wine,
        The murmurous haunt of flies on summer eves.   50

6

Darkling I listen; and, for many a time
    I have been half in love with easeful Death,
Call'd him soft names in many a mused rhyme,
    To take into the air my quiet breath;

Now more than ever seems it rich to die,   55
  To cease upon the midnight with no pain,
    While thou art pouring forth thy soul abroad
      In such an ecstasy!
    Still wouldst thou sing, and I have ears in vain—
      To thy high requiem become a sod.   60

7

Thou wast not born for death, immortal Bird!
  No hungry generations tread thee down;
The voice I hear this passing night was heard
  In ancient days by emperor and clown:
Perhaps the self-same song that found a path   65
  Through the sad heart of Ruth, when, sick for home,
    She stood in tears amid the alien corn;
      The same that oft-times hath
    Charm'd magic casements, opening on the foam
      Of perilous seas, in faery lands forlorn.   70

8

Forlorn! the very word is like a bell
  To toll me back from thee to my sole self!
Adieu! the fancy cannot cheat so well
  As she is fam'd to do, deceiving elf.
Adieu! adieu! thy plaintive anthem fades   75
  Past the near meadows, over the still stream,
    Up the hill-side; and now 'tis buried deep
      In the next valley-glades:
    Was it a vision, or a waking dream?
      Fled is that music:—Do I wake or sleep?   80

ODE ON A GRECIAN URN

1

Thou still unravish'd bride of quietness,
    Thou foster-child of silence and slow time,
Sylvan historian, who canst thus express
    A flowery tale more sweetly than our rhyme:
What leaf-fring'd legend haunts about thy shape   5
    Of deities or mortals, or of both,
        In Tempe or the dales of Arcady?
What men or gods are these? What maidens loth?
    What mad pursuit? What struggle to escape?
        What pipes and timbrels? What wild ecstasy?   10

2

Heard melodies are sweet, but those unheard
    Are sweeter; therefore, ye soft pipes, play on;
Not to the sensual ear, but, more endear'd,
    Pipe to the spirit ditties of no tone:
Fair youth, beneath the trees, thou canst not leave   15
    Thy song, nor ever can those trees be bare;
        Bold Lover, never, never canst thou kiss,
Though winning near the goal—yet, do not grieve;
    She cannot fade, though thou has not thy bliss,
        For ever wilt thou love, and she be fair!   20

3

Ah, happy, happy boughs! that cannot shed
    Your leaves, nor ever bid the Spring adieu;
And, happy melodist, unwearied,
    For ever piping songs for ever new;
More happy love! more happy, happy love!   25
    For ever warm and still to be enjoy'd,
        For ever panting, and for ever young;

All breathing human passion far above,
 That leaves a heart high-sorrowful and cloy'd,
  A burning forehead, and a parching tongue. 30

4

Who are these coming to the sacrifice?
 To what green altar, O mysterious priest,
Lead'st thou that heifer lowing at the skies,
 And all her silken flanks with garlands drest?
What little town by river or sea shore, 35
 Or mountain-built with peaceful citadel,
  Is emptied of this folk, this pious morn?
And, little town, thy streets for evermore
 Will silent be; and not a soul to tell
  Why thou art desolate, can e'er return. 40

5

O Attic shape! Fair attitude! with brede
 Of marble men and maidens overwrought,
With forest branches and the trodden weed;
 Thou, silent form, dost tease us out of thought
As doth eternity: Cold Pastoral! 45
 When old age shall this generation waste,
  Thou shalt remain, in midst of other woe
Than ours, a friend to man, to whom thou say'st,
 'Beauty is truth, truth beauty,'—that is all
  Ye know on earth, and all ye need to know. 50

77

ODE TO PSYCHE

O GODDESS! hear these tuneless numbers, wrung
   By sweet enforcement and remembrance dear,
And pardon that thy secrets should be sung
   Even into thine own soft-conched ear:
Surely I dreamt to-day, or did I see   5
   The winged Psyche with awaken'd eyes?
I wander'd in a forest thoughtlessly,
   And, on the sudden, fainting with surprise,
Saw two fair creatures, couched side by side
   In deepest grass, beneath the whisp'ring roof   10
   Of leaves and trembled blossoms, where there ran
       A brooklet, scarce espied:

'Mid hush'd, cool-rooted flowers, fragrant-eyed,
   Blue, silver-white, and budded Tyrian,
They lay calm-breathing on the bedded grass;   15
   Their arms embraced, and their pinions too;
   Their lips touch'd not, but had not bade adieu,
As if disjoined by soft-handed slumber,
And ready still past kisses to outnumber
   At tender eye-dawn of aurorean love: 20
       The winged boy I knew;
   But who wast thou, O happy, happy dove?
       His Psyche true!

O latest born and loveliest vision far
   Of all Olympus' faded hierarchy!   25
Fairer than Phoebe's sapphire-region'd star,
   Or Vesper, amorous glow-worm of the sky;
Fairer than these, though temple thou hast none,
   Nor altar heap'd with flowers;

Nor virgin-choir to make delicious moan   30
    Upon the midnight hours;
No voice, no lute, no pipe, no incense sweet
  From chain-swung censer teeming;
No shrine, no grove, no oracle, no heat
    Of pale-mouth'd prophet dreaming.   35

O brightest! though too late for antique vows,
  Too, too late for the fond believing lyre,
When holy were the haunted forest boughs,
  Holy the air, the water, and the fire;
Yet even in these days so far retir'd   40
  From happy pieties, thy lucent fans,
  Fluttering among the faint Olympians,
I see, and sing, by my own eyes inspired.
So let me be thy choir, and make a moan
    Upon the midnight hours;   45
Thy voice, thy lute, thy pipe, thy incense sweet
  From swinged censer teeming;
Thy shrine, thy grove, thy oracle, thy heat
  Of pale-mouth'd prophet dreaming.

Yes, I will be thy priest, and build a fane   50
  In some untrodden region of my mind,
Where branched thoughts, new grown with pleasant
    pain,
  Instead of pines shall murmur in the wind:
Far, far around shall those dark-cluster'd trees
  Fledge the wild-ridged mountains steep by steep; 55
And there by zephyrs, streams, and birds, and bees,
  The moss-lain Dryads shall be lull'd to sleep;
And in the midst of this wide quietness
A rosy sanctuary will I dress

With the wreath'd trellis of a working brain,   60
    With buds, and bells, and stars without a name,
With all the gardener Fancy e'er could feign,
    Who breeding flowers, will never breed the same:
And there shall be for thee all soft delight
    That shadowy thought can win,   65
A bright torch, and a casement ope at night,
    To let the warm Love in!

FANCY

Ever let the Fancy roam,
Pleasure never is at home:
At a touch sweet Pleasure melteth,
Like to bubbles when rain pelteth;
Then let winged Fancy wander   5
Through the thought still spread beyond her:
Open wide the mind's cage-door,
She'll dart forth, and cloudward soar.
O sweet Fancy! let her loose;
Summer's joys are spoilt by use,   10
And the enjoying of the Spring
Fades as does its blossoming;
Autumn's red-lipp'd fruitage too,
Blushing through the mist and dew,
Cloys with tasting: What do then?   15
Sit thee by the ingle, when
The sear faggot blazes bright,
Spirit of a winter's night;
When the soundless earth is muffled,
And the caked snow is shuffled   20
From the ploughboy's heavy shoon;
When the Night doth meet the Noon
In a dark conspiracy
To banish Even from her sky.
Sit thee there, and send abroad,   25
With a mind self-overaw'd,
Fancy, high-commission'd:—send her!
She has vassals to attend her:
She will bring, in spite of frost,
Beauties that the earth hath lost;   30
She will bring thee, all together,
All delights of summer weather;
All the buds and bells of May,
From dewy sward or thorny spray

All the heaped Autumn's wealth,   35
With a still, mysterious stealth:
She will mix these pleasures up
Like three fit wines in a cup,
And thou shalt quaff it:—thou shalt hear
Distant harvest-carols clear;   40
Rustle of the reaped corn;
Sweet birds antheming the morn:
And, in the same moment—hark!
'Tis the early April lark,
Or the rooks, with busy caw,   45
Foraging for sticks and straw.
Thou shalt, at one glance, behold
The daisy and the marigold;
White-plum'd lilies, and the first
Hedge-grown primrose that hath burst;   50
Shaded hyacinth, alway
Sapphire queen of the mid-May;
And every leaf, and every flower
Pearled with the self-same shower.
Thou shalt see the field-mouse peep   55
Meagre from its celled sleep;
And the snake all winter-thin
Cast on sunny bank its skin;
Freckled nest-eggs thou shalt see
Hatching in the hawthorn-tree,   60
When the hen-bird's wing doth rest
Quiet on her mossy nest;
Then the hurry and alarm
When the bee-hive casts its swarm;   65
Acorns ripe down-pattering,
While the autumn breezes sing.

    Oh, sweet Fancy! let her loose;
Every thing is spoilt by use:
Where's the cheek that doth not fade,

Too much gaz'd at? Where's the maid   70
Whose lip mature is ever new?
Where's the eye, however blue,
Doth not weary? Where's the face
One would meet in every place?
Where's the voice, however soft,   75
One would hear so very oft?
At a touch sweet Pleasure melteth
Like to bubbles when rain pelteth.
Let, then, winged Fancy find
Thee a mistress to thy mind: 80
Dulcet-eyed as Ceres' daughter,
Ere the God of Torment taught her
How to frown and how to chide;
With a waist and with a side
White as Hebe's, when her zone   85
Slipt its golden clasp, and down
Fell her kirtle to her feet,
While she held the goblet sweet,
And Jove grew languid.—Break the mesh
Of the Fancy's silken leash;   90
Quickly break her prison-string
And such joys as these she'll bring.—
Let the winged Fancy roam
Pleasure never is at home.

ODE

BARDS of Passion and of Mirth,
Ye have left your souls on earth!
Have ye souls in heaven too,
Double-lived in regions new?
Yes, and those of heaven commune   5
With the spheres of sun and moon;
With the noise of fountains wond'rous,

And the parle of voices thund'rous;
With the whisper of heaven's trees
And one another, in soft ease   10
Seated on Elysian lawns
Brows'd by none but Dian's fawns
Underneath large blue-bells tented,
Where the daisies are rose-scented,
And the rose herself has got   15
Perfume which on earth is not;
Where the nightingale doth sing
Not a senseless, tranced thing,
But divine melodious truth;
Philosophic numbers smooth;   20
Tales and golden histories
Of heaven and its mysteries.

Thus ye live on high, and then
On the earth ye live again;
And the souls ye left behind you   25
Teach us, here, the way to find you,
Where your other souls are joying,
Never slumber'd, never cloying.
Here, your earth-born souls still speak
To mortals, of their little week;   30
Of their sorrows and delights;
Of their passions and their spites;
Of their glory and their shame;
What doth strengthen and what maim.
Thus ye teach us, every day,   35
Wisdom, though fled far away.

Bards of Passion and of Mirth,
Ye have left your souls on earth!
Ye have souls in heaven too,
Double-lived in regions new!   40

LINES ON THE MERMAID TAVERN

SOULS of Poets dead and gone,
What Elysium have ye known,
Happy field or mossy cavern,
Choicer than the Mermaid Tavern?
Have ye tippled drink more fine   5
Than mine host's Canary wine?
Or are fruits of Paradise
Sweeter than those dainty pies
Of venison? O generous food!
Drest as though bold Robin Hood   10
Would, with his maid Marian,
Sup and bowse from horn and can.

I have heard that on a day
Mine host's sign-board flew away,
Nobody knew whither, till   15
An astrologer's old quill
To a sheepskin gave the story,
Said he saw you in your glory,
Underneath a new old-sign
Sipping beverage divine,   20
And pledging with contented smack
The Mermaid in the Zodiac.

Souls of Poets dead and gone,
What Elysium have ye known,
Happy field or mossy cavern,   25
Choicer than the Mermaid Tavern?

ROBIN HOOD

TO A FRIEND

No! those days are gone away,
And their hours are old and gray,
And their minutes buried all
Under the down-trodden pall
Of the leaves of many years: 5
Many times have winter's shears,
Frozen North, and chilling East,
Sounded tempests to the feast
Of the forest's whispering fleeces,
Since men knew nor rent nor leases.   10

   No, the bugle sounds no more,
And the twanging bow no more;
Silent is the ivory shrill
Past the heath and up the hill;
There is no mid-forest laugh,   15
Where lone Echo gives the half
To some wight, amaz'd to hear
Jesting, deep in forest drear.

   On the fairest time of June
You may go, with sun or moon,   20
Or the seven stars to light you,
Or the polar ray to right you;
But you never may behold
Little John, or Robin bold;
Never one, of all the clan,   25
Thrumming on an empty can
Some old hunting ditty, while
He doth his green way beguile

To fair hostess Merriment,
Down beside the pasture Trent;   30
For he left the merry tale
Messenger for spicy ale.

    Gone, the merry morris din;
Gone, the song of Gamelyn;
Gone, the tough-belted outlaw   35
Idling in the 'grenè shawe;'
All are gone away and past!
And if Robin should be cast
Sudden from his turfed grave,
And if Marian should have   40
Once again her forest days,
She would weep, and he would craze:
He would swear, for all his oaks,
Fall'n beneath the dockyard strokes,
Have rotted on the briny seas;   45
She would weep that her wild bees
Sang not to her—strange! that honey
Can't be got without hard money!

    So it is: yet let us sing,
Honour to the old bow-string!   50
Honour to the bugle-horn!
Honour to the woods unshorn!
Honour to the Lincoln green!
Honour to the archer keen!
Honour to tight little John,   55
And the horse he rode upon!
Honour to bold Robin Hood,
Sleeping in the underwood!
Honour to maid Marian,
And to all the Sherwood-clan!   60
Though their days have hurried by
Let us two a burden try.

TO AUTUMN

1

SEASON of mists and mellow fruitfulness,
   Close bosom-friend of the maturing sun;
Conspiring with him how to load and bless
   With fruit the vines that round the thatch-eves run;
To bend with apples the moss'd cottage-trees,   5
   And fill all fruit with ripeness to the core;
      To swell the gourd, and plump the hazel shells
With a sweet kernel; to set budding more,
   And still more, later flowers for the bees,
   Until they think warm days will never cease,   10
      For Summer has o'er-brimm'd their clammy cells.

2

Who hath not seen thee oft amid thy store?
   Sometimes whoever seeks abroad may find
Thee sitting careless on a granary floor,
   Thy hair soft-lifted by the winnowing wind;   15
Or on a half-reap'd furrow sound asleep,
   Drows'd with the fume of poppies, while thy hook
      Spares the next swath and all its twined flowers:
And sometimes like a gleaner thou dost keep
   Steady thy laden head across a brook;   20
   Or by a cyder-press, with patient look,
      Thou watchest the last oozings hours by hours.

3

Where are the songs of Spring? Ay, where are they?
   Think not of them, thou hast thy music too,—
While barred clouds bloom the soft-dying day,   25
   And touch the stubble-plains with rosy hue;

Then in a wailful choir the small gnats mourn
   Among the river sallows, borne aloft
     Or sinking as the light wind lives or dies;
And full-grown lambs loud bleat from hilly bourn;   30
   Hedge-crickets sing; and now with treble soft
   The red-breast whistles from a garden-croft;
     And gathering swallows twitter in the skies.

ODE ON MELANCHOLY

1

No, no, go not to Lethe, neither twist
   Wolf's-bane, tight-rooted, for its poisonous wine;
Nor suffer thy pale forehead to be kiss'd
   By nightshade, ruby grape of Proserpine;
Make not your rosary of yew-berries,   5
   Nor let the beetle, nor the death-moth be
     Your mournful Psyche, nor the downy owl
A partner in your sorrow's mysteries;
   For shade to shade will come too drowsily,
     And drown the wakeful anguish of the soul.   10

2

But when the melancholy fit shall fall
   Sudden from heaven like a weeping cloud,
That fosters the droop-headed flowers all,
   And hides the green hill in an April shroud;
Then glut thy sorrow on a morning rose,   15
   Or on the rainbow of the salt sand-wave,
     Or on the wealth of globed peonies;
Or if thy mistress some rich anger shows,
   Emprison her soft hand, and let her rave,
     And feed deep, deep upon her peerless eyes.   20

3

She dwells with Beauty—Beauty that must die;
   And Joy, whose hand is ever at his lips
Bidding adieu; and aching Pleasure nigh,
   Turning to poison while the bee-mouth sips:
Ay, in the very temple of Delight   25
   Veil'd Melancholy has her sovran shrine,
      Though seen of none save him whose strenuous
      tongue
Can burst Joy's grape against his palate fine;
   His soul shall taste the sadness of her might,
      And be among her cloudy trophies hung.   30

HYPERION

A FRAGMENT

BOOK I

DEEP in the shady sadness of a vale
Far sunken from the healthy breath of morn,
Far from the fiery noon, and eve's one star,
Sat gray-hair'd Saturn, quiet as a stone,
Still as the silence round about his lair;   5
Forest on forest hung about his head
Like cloud on cloud. No stir of air was there,
Not so much life as on a summer's day
Robs not one light seed from the feather'd grass,
But where the dead leaf fell, there did it rest.   10
A stream went voiceless by, still deadened more
By reason of his fallen divinity
Spreading a shade: the Naiad 'mid her reeds
Press'd her cold finger closer to her lips.

Along the margin-sand large foot-marks went,   15
No further than to where his feet had stray'd,
And slept there since. Upon the sodden ground
His old right hand lay nerveless, listless, dead,
Unsceptred; and his realmless eyes were closed;
While his bow'd head seem'd list'ning to the Earth,   20
His ancient mother, for some comfort yet.

It seem'd no force could wake him from his place;
But there came one, who with a kindred hand
Touch'd his wide shoulders, after bending low
With reverence, though to one who knew it not.   25
She was a Goddess of the infant world;

91

By her in stature the tall Amazon
Had stood a pigmy's height: she would have ta'en
Achilles by the hair and bent his neck;
Or with a finger stay'd Ixion's wheel.   30
Her face was large as that of Memphian sphinx,
Pedestal'd haply in a palace court,
When sages look'd to Egypt for their lore.
But oh! how unlike marble was that face:
How beautiful, if sorrow had not made   35
Sorrow more beautiful than Beauty's self.
There was a listening fear in her regard,
As if calamity had but begun;
As if the vanward clouds of evil days
Had spent their malice, and the sullen rear   40
Was with its stored thunder labouring up.
One hand she press'd upon that aching spot
Where beats the human heart, as if just there,
Though an immortal, she felt cruel pain:
The other upon Saturn's bended neck   45
She laid, and to the level of his ear
Leaning with parted lips, some words she spake
In solemn tenour and deep organ tone:
Some mourning words, which in our feeble tongue
Would come in these like accents; O how frail   50
To that large utterance of the early Gods!
'Saturn, look up!—though wherefore, poor old King?
'I have no comfort for thee, no not one:
'I cannot say, "Oh wherefore sleepest thou?"
'For heaven is parted from thee, and the earth   55
'Knows thee not, thus afflicted, for a God;
'And ocean too, with all its solemn noise,
'Has from thy sceptre pass'd; and all the air
'Is emptied of thine hoary majesty.
'Thy thunder, conscious of the new command,   60
'Rumbles reluctant o'er our fallen house;
'And thy sharp lightning in unpractised hands

'Scorches and burns our once serene domain.
'O aching time! O moments big as years!
'All as ye pass swell out the monstrous truth,   65
'And press it so upon our weary griefs
'That unbelief has not a space to breathe.
'Saturn, sleep on:—O thoughtless, why did I
'Thus violate thy slumbrous solitude?
'Why should I ope thy melancholy eyes?   70
'Saturn, sleep on! while at thy feet I weep.'

    As when, upon a tranced summer-night,
Those green-rob'd senators of mighty woods,
Tall oaks, branch-charmed by the earnest stars,
Dream, and so dream all night without a stir,   75
Save from one gradual solitary gust
Which comes upon the silence, and dies off,
As if the ebbing air had but one wave;
So came these words and went; the while in tears
She touch'd her fair large forehead to the ground,   80
Just where her falling hair might be outspread
A soft and silken mat for Saturn's feet.
One moon, with alteration slow, had shed
Her silver seasons four upon the night,
And still these two were postured motionless,   85
Like natural sculpture in cathedral cavern;
The frozen God still couchant on the earth,
And the sad Goddess weeping at his feet:
Until at length old Saturn lifted up
His faded eyes, and saw his kingdom gone,   90
And all the gloom and sorrow of the place,
And that fair kneeling Goddess; and then spake,
As with a palsied tongue, and while his beard
Shook horrid with such aspen-malady:
'O tender spouse of gold Hyperion,   95
'Thea, I feel thee ere I see thy face;
'Look up, and let me see our doom in it;

93

'Look up, and tell me if this feeble shape
'Is Saturn's; tell me, if thou hear'st the voice
'Of Saturn; tell me, if this wrinkling brow,   100
'Naked and bare of its great diadem,
'Peers like the front of Saturn. Who had power
'To make me desolate? whence came the strength?
'How was it nurtur'd to such bursting forth,
'While Fate seem'd strangled in my nervous grasp?   105
'But it is so; and I am smother'd up,
'And buried from all godlike exercise
'Of influence benign on planets pale,
'Of admonitions to the winds and seas,
'Of peaceful sway above man's harvesting,   110
'And all those acts which Deity supreme
'Doth ease its heart of love in.—I am gone
'Away from my own bosom: I have left
'My strong identity, my real self,
'Somewhere between the throne, and where I sit   115
'Here on this spot of earth. Search, Thea, search!
'Open thine eyes eterne, and sphere them round
'Upon all space: space starr'd, and lorn of light;
'Space region'd with life-air; and barren void;
'Spaces of fire, and all the yawn of hell.—   120
'Search, Thea, search! and tell me, if thou seest
'A certain shape or shadow, making way
'With wings or chariot fierce to repossess
'A heaven he lost erewhile: it must—it must
'Be of ripe progress—Saturn must be King.   125
'Yes, there must be a golden victory;
'There must be Gods thrown down, and trumpets
    blown
'Of triumph calm, and hymns of festival
'Upon the gold clouds metropolitan,
'Voices of soft proclaim, and silver stir   130
'Of strings in hollow shells; and there shall be
'Beautiful things made new, for the surprise

'Of the sky-children; I will give command:
'Thea! Thea! Thea! where is Saturn?'

    This passion lifted him upon his feet,   135
And made his hands to struggle in the air,
His Druid locks to shake and ooze with sweat,
His eyes to fever out, his voice to cease.
He stood, and heard not Thea's sobbing deep;
A little time, and then again he snatch'd   140
Utterance thus.—'But cannot I create?
'Cannot I form? Cannot I fashion forth
'Another world, another universe,
'To overbear and crumble this to nought?
'Where is another Chaos? Where?'—That word   145
Found way unto Olympus, and made quake
The rebel three.—Thea was startled up,
And in her bearing was a sort of hope,
As thus she quick-voic'd spake, yet full of awe.

    'This cheers our fallen house: come to our friends, 150
'O Saturn! come away, and give them heart;
'I know the covert, for thence came I hither.'
Thus brief; then with beseeching eyes she went
With backward footing through the shade a space:
He follow'd, and she turn'd to lead the way   155
Through aged boughs, that yielded like the mist
Which eagles cleave upmounting from their nest.

    Meanwhile in other realms big tears were shed,
More sorrow like to this, and such like woe,
Too huge for mortal tongue or pen of scribe: 160
The Titans fierce, self-hid, or prison-bound,
Groan'd for the old allegiance once more,
And listen'd in sharp pain for Saturn's voice.
But one of the whole mammoth-brood still kept
His sov'reignty, and rule, and majesty;—   165

Blazing Hyperion on his orbed fire
Still sat, still snuff'd the incense, teeming up
From man to the sun's God; yet unsecure:
For as among us mortals omens drear
Fright and perplex, so also shuddered he—   170
Not at dog's howl, or gloom-bird's hated screech,
Or the familiar visiting of one
Upon the first toll of his passing-bell,
Or prophesyings of the midnight lamp;
But horrors, portion'd to a giant nerve,   175
Oft made Hyperion ache. His palace bright
Bastion'd with pyramids of glowing gold,
And touch'd with shade of bronzed obelisks,
Glar'd a blood-red through all its thousand courts,
Arches, and domes, and fiery galleries;   180
And all its curtains of Aurorian clouds
Flush'd angerly: while sometimes eagle's wings,
Unseen before by Gods or wondering men,
Darken'd the place; and neighing steeds were heard,
Not heard before by Gods or wondering men.   185
Also, when he would taste the spicy wreaths
Of incense, breath'd aloft from sacred hills,
Instead of sweets, his ample palate took
Savour of poisonous brass and metal sick:
And so, when harbour'd in the sleepy west,   190
After the full completion of fair day,—
For rest divine upon exalted couch
And slumber in the arms of melody,
He pac'd away the pleasant hours of ease
With stride colossal, on from hall to hall;   195
While far within each aisle and deep recess,
His winged minions in close clusters stood,
Amaz'd and full of fear; like anxious men
Who on wide plains gather in panting troops,
When earthquakes jar their battlements and towers.   200
Even now, while Saturn, rous'd from icy trance,

Went step for step with Thea through the woods,
Hyperion, leaving twilight in the rear,
Came slope upon the threshold of the west;
Then, as was wont, his palace-door flew ope   205
In smoothest silence, save what solemn tubes,
Blown by the serious Zephyrs, gave of sweet
And wandering sounds, slow-breathed melodies;
And like a rose in vermeil tint and shape,
In fragrance soft, and coolness to the eye,   210
That inlet to severe magnificence
Stood full blown, for the God to enter in.

He enter'd, but he enter'd full of wrath;
His flaming robes stream'd out beyond his heels,
And gave a roar, as if of earthly fire,   215
That scar'd away the meek ethereal Hours
And made their dove-wings tremble. On he flared,
From stately nave to nave, from vault to vault,
Through bowers of fragrant and enwreathed light,
And diamond-paved lustrous long arcades,   220
Until he reach'd the great main cupola;
There standing fierce beneath, he stampt his foot,
And from the basements deep to the high towers
Jarr'd his own golden region; and before
The quavering thunder thereupon had ceas'd,   225
His voice leapt out, despite of godlike curb,
To this result: 'O dreams of day and night!
'O monstrous forms! O effigies of pain!
'O spectres busy in a cold, cold gloom!
'O lank-eared Phantoms of black-weeded pools!   230
'Why do I know ye? why have I seen ye? why
'Is my eternal essence thus distraught
'To see and to behold these horrors new?
'Saturn is fallen, am I too to fall?
'Am I to leave this haven of my rest,   235
'This cradle of my glory, this soft clime,

'This calm luxuriance of blissful light,
'These crystalline pavilions, and pure fanes,
'Of all my lucent empire? It is left
'Deserted, void, nor any haunt of mine.   240
'The blaze, the splendor, and the symmetry,
'I cannot see—but darkness, death and darkness.
'Even here, into my centre of repose,
'The shady visions come to domineer,
'Insult, and blind, and stifle up my pomp.—   245
'Fall!—No, by Tellus and her briny robes!
'Over the fiery frontier of my realms
'I will advance a terrible right arm
'Shall scare that infant thunderer, rebel Jove,
'And bid old Saturn take his throne again.'—   250
He spake, and ceas'd, the while a heavier threat
Held struggle with his throat but came not forth;
For as in theatres of crowded men
Hubbub increases more they call out 'Hush!'
So at Hyperion's words the Phantoms pale   255
Bestirr'd themselves, thrice horrible and cold;
And from the mirror'd level where he stood
A mist arose, as from a scummy marsh.
At this, through all his bulk an agony
Crept gradual, from the feet unto the crown,   260
Like a lithe serpent vast and muscular
Making slow way, with head and neck convuls'd
From over-strained might. Releas'd, he fled
To the eastern gates, and full six dewy hours
Before the dawn in season due should blush,   265
He breath'd fierce breath against the sleepy portals,
Clear'd them of heavy vapours, burst them wide
Suddenly on the ocean's chilly streams.
The planet orb of fire, whereon he rode
Each day from east to west the heavens through,   270
Spun round in sable curtaining of clouds;
Not therefore veiled quite, blindfold, and hid,

But ever and anon the glancing spheres,
Circles, and arcs, and broad-belting colure,
Glow'd through, and wrought upon the muffling dark 275
Sweet-shaped lightnings from the nadir deep
Up to the zenith,—hieroglyphics old,
Which sages and keen-eyed astrologers
Then living on the earth, with labouring thought
Won from the gaze of many centuries: 280
Now lost, save what we find on remnants huge
Of stone, or marble swart; their import gone,
Their wisdom long since fled.—Two wings this orb
Possess'd for glory, two fair argent wings,
Ever exalted at the God's approach: 285
And now, from forth the gloom their plumes immense
Rose, one by one, till all outspreaded were;
While still the dazzling globe maintain'd eclipse,
Awaiting for Hyperion's command.
Fain would he have commanded, fain took throne   290
And bid the day begin, if but for change.
He might not:—No, though a primeval God:
The sacred seasons might not be disturb'd.
Therefore the operations of the dawn
Stay'd in their birth, even as here 'tis told.   295
Those silver wings expanded sisterly,
Eager to sail their orb; the porches wide
Open'd upon the dusk demesnes of night
And the bright Titan, phrenzied with new woes,
Unus'd to bend, by hard compulsion bent   300
His spirit to the sorrow of the time;
And all along a dismal rack of clouds,
Upon the boundaries of day and night,
He stretch'd himself in grief and radiance faint.
There as he lay, the Heaven with its stars   305
Look'd down on him with pity, and the voice
Of Cœlus, from the universal space,
Thus whisper'd low and solemn in his ear.

'O brightest of my children dear, earth-born
'And sky-engendered, Son of Mysteries   310
'All unrevealed even to the powers
'Which met at thy creating; at whose joys
'And palpitations sweet, and pleasures soft,
'I, Cœlus, wonder, how they came and whence;
'And at the fruits thereof what shapes they be, 315
'Distinct, and visible; symbols divine,
'Manifestations of that beauteous life
'Diffus'd unseen throughout eternal space:
'Of these new-form'd art thou, oh brightest child!
'Of these, thy brethren and the Goddesses!   320
'There is sad feud among ye, and rebellion
'Of son against his sire. I saw him fall,
'I saw my first-born tumbled from his throne!
'To me his arms were spread, to me his voice
'Found way from forth the thunders round his head! 325
'Pale wox I, and in vapours hid my face.
'Art thou, too, near such doom? vague fear there is:
'For I have seen my sons most unlike Gods.
'Divine ye were created, and divine
'In sad demeanour, solemn, undisturb'd,   330
'Unruffled, like high Gods, ye liv'd and ruled:
'Now I behold in you fear, hope, and wrath;
'Actions of rage and passion; even as
'I see them, on the mortal world beneath,
'In men who die.—This is the grief, O Son!   335
'Sad sign of ruin, sudden dismay, and fall!
'Yet do thou strive; as thou art capable,
'As thou canst move about, an evident God;
'And canst oppose to each malignant hour
'Ethereal presence:—I am but a voice;   340
'My life is but the life of winds and tides,
'No more than winds and tides can I avail:—
'But thou canst.—Be thou therefore in the van
'Of circumstance; yea, seize the arrow's barb

'Before the tense string murmur.—To the earth!   345
'For there thou wilt find Saturn, and his woes.
'Meantime I will keep watch on thy bright sun,
'And of thy seasons be a careful nurse.'—
Ere half this region-whisper had come down,
Hyperion arose, and on the stars   350
Lifted his curved lids, and kept them wide
Until it ceas'd; and still he kept them wide:
And still they were the same bright, patient stars.
Then with a slow incline of his broad breast,
Like to a diver in the pearly seas,   355
Forward he stoop'd over the airy shore,
And plung'd all noiseless into the deep night.

HYPERION—BOOK II

JUST at the self-same beat of Time's wide wings
Hyperion slid into the rustled air,
And Saturn gain'd with Thea that sad place
Where Cybele and the bruised Titans mourn'd.
It was a den where no insulting light   5
Could glimmer on their tears; where their own groans
They felt, but heard not, for the solid roar
Of thunderous waterfalls and torrents hoarse,
Pouring a constant bulk, uncertain where.
Crag jutting forth to crag, and rocks that seem'd   10
Ever as if just rising from a sleep,
Forehead to forehead held their monstrous horns;
And thus in thousand hugest phantasies
Made a fit roofing to this nest of woe.
Instead of thrones, hard flint they sat upon,   15
Couches of rugged stone, and slaty ridge
Stubborn'd with iron. All were not assembled:
Some chain'd in torture, and some wandering.

Cœus, and Gyges, and Briareüs,
Typhon, and Dolor, and Porphyrion,   20
With many more, the brawniest in assault,
Were pent in regions of laborious breath;
Dungeon'd in opaque element, to keep
Their clenched teeth still clench'd, and all their limbs
Lock'd up like veins of metal, crampt and screw'd;   25
Without a motion, save of their big hearts
Heaving in pain, and horribly convuls'd
With sanguine feverous boiling gurge of pulse.
Mnemosyne was straying in the world;
Far from her moon had Phœbe wandered;   30
And many else were free to roam abroad,
But for the main, here found they covert drear.
Scarce images of life, one here, one there,
Lay vast and edgeways; like a dismal cirque
Of Druid stones, upon a forlorn moor,   35
When the chill rain begins at shut of eve,
In dull November, and their chancel vault,
The Heaven itself, is blinded throughout night.
Each one kept shroud, nor to his neighbour gave
Or word, or look, or action of despair.   40
Creüs was one; his ponderous iron mace
Lay by him, and a shatter'd rib of rock
Told of his rage, ere he thus sank and pined.
Iäpetus another; in his grasp,
A serpent's plashy neck; its barbed tongue   45
Squeez'd from the gorge, and all its uncurl'd length
Dead; and because the creature could not spit
Its poison in the eyes of conquering Jove.
Next Cottus: prone he lay, chin uppermost,
As though in pain; for still upon the flint   50
He ground severe his skull, with open mouth
And eyes at horrid working. Nearest him
Asia, born of most enormous Caf,
Who cost her mother Tellus keener pangs,

Though feminine, than any of her sons: 55
More thought than woe was in her dusky face,
For she was prophesying of her glory;
And in her wide imagination stood
Palm-shaded temples, and high rival fanes,
By Oxus or in Ganges' sacred isles.   60
Even as Hope upon her anchor leans,
So leant she, not so fair, upon a tusk
Shed from the broadest of her elephants.
Above her, on a crag's uneasy shelve,
Upon his elbow rais'd, all prostrate else,   65
Shadow'd Enceladus; once tame and mild
As grazing ox unworried in the meads;
Now tiger-passion'd, lion-thoughted, wroth,
He meditated, plotted, and even now
Was hurling mountains in that second war,   70
Not long delay'd, that scar'd the younger Gods
To hide themselves in forms of beast and bird.
Not far hence Atlas; and beside him prone
Phorcus, the sire of Gorgons. Neighbour'd close
Oceanus, and Tethys, in whose lap   75
Sobb'd Clymene among her tangled hair.
In midst of all lay Themis, at the feet
Of Ops the queen all clouded round from sight;
No shape distinguishable, more than when
Thick night confounds the pine-tops with the clouds: 80
And many else whose names may not be told.
For when the Muse's wings are air-ward spread,
Who shall delay her flight? And she must chaunt
Of Saturn, and his guide, who now had climb'd
With damp and slippery footing from a depth   85
More horrid still. Above a sombre cliff
Their heads appear'd, and up their stature grew
Till on the level height their steps found ease:
Then Thea spread abroad her trembling arms
Upon the precincts of this nest of pain,   90

And sidelong fix'd her eye on Saturn's face:
There saw she direst strife; the supreme God
At war with all the frailty of grief,
Of rage, of fear, anxiety, revenge,
Remorse, spleen, hope, but most of all despair.   95
Against these plagues he strove in vain; for Fate
Had pour'd a mortal oil upon his head,
A disanointing poison: so that Thea
Affrighted, kept her still, and let him pass
First onwards in, among the fallen tribe.   100

As with us mortal men, the laden heart
Is persecuted more, and fever'd more,
When it is nighing to the mournful house
Where other hearts are sick of the same bruise;
So Saturn, as he walk'd into the midst,   105
Felt faint, and would have sunk among the rest,
But that he met Enceladus's eye,
Whose mightiness, and awe of him, at once
Came like an inspiration; and he shouted,
'Titans, behold your God!' at which some groan'd;   110
Some started on their feet; some also shouted;
Some wept, some wail'd, all bow'd with reverence;
And Ops, uplifting her black folded veil,
Show'd her pale cheeks, and all her forehead wan,
Her eye-brows thin and jet, and hollow eyes.   115
There is a roaring in the bleak-grown pines
When Winter lifts his voice; there is a noise
Among immortals when a God gives sign,
With hushing finger, how he means to load
His tongue with the full weight of utterless thought,   120
With thunder, and with music, and with pomp:
Such noise is like the roar of bleak-grown pines;
Which, when it ceases in this mountain'd world,
No other sound succeeds; but ceasing here,
Among these fallen, Saturn's voice therefrom   125

Grew up like organ, that begins anew
Its strain, when other harmonies, stopt short,
Leave the dinn'd air vibrating silverly.
Thus grew it up—'Not in my own sad breast,
'Which is its own great judge and searcher out,   130
'Can I find reason why ye should be thus:
'Not in the legends of the first of days,
'Studied from that old spirit-leaved book
'Which starry Uranus with finger bright
'Sav'd from the shores of darkness, when the waves   135
'Low-ebb'd still hid it up in shallow gloom;—
'And the which book ye know I ever kept
'For my firm-based footstool:—Ah, infirm!
'Not there, nor in sign, symbol, or portent
'Of element, earth, water, air, and fire,—   140
'At war, at peace, or inter-quarreling
'One against one, or two, or three, or all
'Each several one against the other three,
'As fire with air loud warring when rain-floods
'Drown both, and press them both against earth's face, 145
'Where, finding sulphur, a quadruple wrath
'Unhinges the poor world;—not in that strife,
'Wherefrom I take strange lore, and read it deep,
'Can I find reason why ye should be thus:
'No, no-where can unriddle, though I search,   150
'And pore on Nature's universal scroll
'Even to swooning, why ye, Divinities,
'The first-born of all shap'd and palpable Gods,
'Should cower beneath what, in comparison,
'Is untremendous might. Yet ye are here,   155
'O'erwhelm'd, and spurn'd, and batter'd, ye are here!
'O Titans, shall I say "Arise!"—Ye groan:
'Shall I say "Crouch!"—Ye groan. What can I then?
'O Heaven wide! O unseen parent dear!
'What can I? Tell me, all ye brethren Gods,   160
'How we can war, how engine our great wrath!

'O speak your counsel now, for Saturn's ear
'Is all a-hunger'd. Thou, Oceanus,
'Ponderest high and deep; and in thy face
'I see, astonied, that severe content   165
'Which comes of thought and musing: give us help!'

So ended Saturn; and the God of the Sea,
Sophist and sage, from no Athenian grove,
But cogitation in his watery shades,
Arose, with locks not oozy, and began,   170
In murmurs, which his first-endeavouring tongue
Caught infant-like from the far-foamed sands.
'O ye, whom wrath consumes! who, passion-stung,
'Writhe at defeat, and nurse your agonies!
'Shut up your senses, stifle up your ears,   175
'My voice is not a bellows unto ire.
'Yet listen, ye who will, whilst I bring proof
'How ye, perforce, must be content to stoop:
'And in the proof much comfort will I give,
'If ye will take that comfort in its truth.   180
'We fall by course of Nature's law, not force
'Of thunder, or of Jove. Great Saturn, thou
'Hast sifted well the atom-universe;
'But for this reason, that thou art the King,
'And only blind from sheer supremacy,   185
'One avenue was shaded from thine eyes,
'Through which I wandered to eternal truth.
'And first, as thou wast not the first of powers,
'So art thou not the last; it cannot be:
'Thou art not the beginning nor the end.   190
'From Chaos and parental Darkness came
'Light, the first fruits of that intestine broil,
'That sullen ferment, which for wondrous ends
'Was ripening in itself. The ripe hour came,
'And with it Light, and Light, engendering   195
'Upon its own producer, forthwith touch'd

'The whole enormous matter into life.
'Upon that very hour, our parentage,
'The Heavens and the Earth, were manifest:
'Then thou first-born, and we the giant-race,   200
'Found ourselves ruling new and beauteous realms.
'Now comes the pain of truth, to whom 'tis pain;
'O folly! for to bear all naked truths,
'And to envisage circumstance, all calm,
'That is the top of sovereignty. Mark well!   205
'As Heaven and Earth are fairer, fairer far
'Than Chaos and blank Darkness, though once
        chiefs;
'And as we show beyond that Heaven and Earth
'In form and shape compact and beautiful,
'In will, in action free, companionship,   210
'And thousand other signs of purer life;
'So on our heels a fresh perfection treads,
'A power more strong in beauty, born of us
'And fated to excel us, as we pass
'In glory that old Darkness: nor are we   215
'Thereby more conquer'd, than by us the rule
'Of shapeless Chaos. Say, doth the dull soil
'Quarrel with the proud forests it hath fed,
'And feedeth still, more comely than itself?
'Can it deny the chiefdom of green groves?   220
'Or shall the tree be envious of the dove
'Because it cooeth, and hath snowy wings
'To wander wherewithal and find its joys?
'We are such forest-trees, and our fair boughs
'Have bred forth, not pale solitary doves,   225
'But eagles golden-feather'd, who do tower
'Above us in their beauty, and must reign
'In right thereof; for 'tis the eternal law
'That first in beauty should be first in might:
'Yea, by that law, another race may drive   230
'Our conquerors to mourn as we do now.

'Have ye beheld the young God of the Seas,
'My dispossessor? Have ye seen his face?
'Have ye beheld his chariot, foam'd along
'By noble winged creatures he hath made?   235
'I saw him on the calmed waters scud,
'With such a glow of beauty in his eyes,
'That it enforc'd me to bid sad farewell
'To all my empire: farewell sad I took,
'And hither came, to see how dolorous fate   240
'Had wrought upon ye; and how I might best
'Give consolation in this woe extreme.
'Receive the truth, and let it be your balm.'

      Whether through poz'd conviction, or disdain,
They guarded silence, when Oceanus   245
Left murmuring, what deepest thought can tell?
But so it was, none answer'd for a space,
Save one whom none regarded, Clymene;
And yet she answer'd not, only complain'd,
With hectic lips, and eyes up-looking mild,   250
Thus wording timidly among the fierce:
'O Father, I am here the simplest voice,
'And all my knowledge is that joy is gone,
'And this thing woe crept in among our hearts,
'There to remain for ever, as I fear: 255
'I would not bode of evil, if I thought
'So weak a creature could turn off the help
'Which by just right should come of mighty Gods;
'Yet let me tell my sorrow, let me tell
'Of what I heard, and how it made me weep,   260
'And know that we had parted from all hope.
'I stood upon a shore, a pleasant shore,
'Where a sweet clime was breathed from a land
'Of fragrance, quietness, and trees, and flowers.
'Full of calm joy it was, as I of grief;   265
'Too full of joy and soft delicious warmth;

'So that I felt a movement in my heart
'To chide, and to reproach that solitude
'With songs of misery, music of our woes;
'And sat me down, and took a mouthed shell   270
'And murmur'd into it, and made melody—
'O melody no more! for while I sang,
'And with poor skill let pass into the breeze
'The dull shell's echo, from a bowery strand
'Just opposite, an island of the sea,   275
'There came enchantment with the shifting wind,
'That did both drown and keep alive my ears.
'I threw my shell away upon the sand,
'And a wave fill'd it, as my sense was fill'd
'With that new blissful golden melody.   280
'A living death was in each gush of sounds,
'Each family of rapturous hurried notes,
'That fell, one after one, yet all at once,
'Like pearl beads dropping sudden from their string:
'And then another, then another strain,   285
'Each like a dove leaving its olive perch,
'With music wing'd instead of silent plumes,
'To hover round my head, and make me sick
'Of joy and grief at once. Grief overcame,
'And I was stopping up my frantic ears,   290
'When, past all hindrance of my trembling hands,
'A voice came sweeter, sweeter than all tune,
'And still it cried, "Apollo! young Apollo!
' "The morning-bright Apollo! young Apollo!"
'I fled, it follow'd me, and cried "Apollo!"   295
'O Father, and O Brethren, had ye felt
'Those pains of mine; O Saturn, hadst thou felt,
'Ye would not call this too indulged tongue
'Presumptuous, in thus venturing to be heard.'

    So far her voice flow'd on, like timorous brook   300
That, lingering along a pebbled coast,

Doth fear to meet the sea: but sea it met,
And shudder'd; for the overwhelming voice
Of huge Enceladus swallow'd it in wrath:
The ponderous syllables, like sullen waves   305
In the half-glutted hollows of reef-rocks,
Came booming thus, while still upon his arm
He lean'd; not rising, from supreme contempt.
'Or shall we listen to the over-wise,
'Or to the over-foolish, Giant-Gods?   310
'Not thunderbolt on thunderbolt, till all
'That rebel Jove's whole armoury were spent,
'Not world on world upon these shoulders piled,
'Could agonize me more than baby-words
'In midst of this dethronement horrible.   315
'Speak! roar! shout! yell! ye sleepy Titans all.
'Do ye forget the blows, the buffets vile?
'Are ye not smitten by a youngling arm?
'Dost thou forget, sham Monarch of the Waves,
'Thy scalding in the seas? What, have I rous'd   320
'Your spleens with so few simple words as these?
'O joy! for now I see ye are not lost:
'O joy! for now I see a thousand eyes
'Wide glaring for revenge!'—As this he said,
He lifted up his stature vast, and stood,   325
Still without intermission speaking thus:
'Now ye are flames, I'll tell you how to burn,
'And purge the ether of our enemies;
'How to feed fierce the crooked stings of fire,
'And singe away the swollen clouds of Jove,   330
'Stifling that puny essence in its tent.
'O let him feel the evil he hath done;
'For though I scorn Oceanus's lore,
'Much pain have I for more than loss of realms:
'The days of peace and slumberous calm are fled;   335
'Those days, all innocent of scathing war,
'When all the fair Existences of heaven

'Came open-eyed to guess what we would speak:—
'That was before our brows were taught to frown,
'Before our lips knew else but solemn sounds;   340
'That was before we knew the winged thing,
'Victory, might be lost, or might be won.
'And be ye mindful that Hyperion,
'Our brightest brother, still is undisgraced—
'Hyperion, lo! his radiance is here!'   345

    All eyes were on Enceladus's face,
And they beheld, while still Hyperion's name
Flew from his lips up to the vaulted rocks,
A pallid gleam across his features stern:
Not savage, for he saw full many a God   350
Wroth as himself. He look'd upon them all,
And in each face he saw a gleam of light,
But splendider in Saturn's, whose hoar locks
Shone like the bubbling foam about a keel
When the prow sweeps into a midnight cove.   355
In pale and silver silence they remain'd,
Till suddenly a splendour, like the morn,
Pervaded all the beetling gloomy steeps,
All the sad spaces of oblivion,
And every gulf, and every chasm old,   360
And every height, and every sullen depth,
Voiceless, or hoarse with loud tormented streams:
And all the everlasting cataracts,
And all the headlong torrents far and near,
Mantled before in darkness and huge shade,   365
Now saw the light and made it terrible.
It was Hyperion:—a granite peak
His bright feet touch'd, and there he stay'd to view
The misery his brilliance had betray'd
To the most hateful seeing of itself.   370
Golden his hair of short Numidian curl,
Regal his shape majestic, a vast shade

In midst of his own brightness, like the bulk
Of Memnon's image at the set of sun
To one who travels from the dusking East: 375
Sighs, too, as mournful as that Memnon's harp
He utter'd, while his hands contemplative
He press'd together, and in silence stood.
Despondence seiz'd again the fallen Gods
At sight of the dejected King of Day,   380
And many hid their faces from the light:
But fierce Enceladus sent forth his eyes
Among the brotherhood; and, at their glare,
Uprose Iäpetus, and Creüs too,
And Phorcus, sea-born, and together strode   385
To where he towered on his eminence.
There those four shouted forth old Saturn's name;
Hyperion from the peak loud answered, 'Saturn!'
Saturn sat near the Mother of the Gods,
In whose face was no joy, though all the Gods   390
Gave from their hollow throats the name of 'Saturn!'

HYPERION—BOOK III

THUS in alternate uproar and sad peace,
Amazed were those Titans utterly.
O leave them, Muse! O leave them to their woes;
For thou art weak to sing such tumults dire:
A solitary sorrow best befits   5
Thy lips, and antheming a lonely grief.
Leave them, O Muse! for thou anon wilt find
Many a fallen old Divinity
Wandering in vain about bewildered shores.
Meantime touch piously the Delphic harp,   10
And not a wind of heaven but will breathe

In aid soft warble from the Dorian flute;
For lo! 'tis for the Father of all verse.
Flush every thing that hath a vermeil hue,
Let the rose glow intense and warm the air, 15
And let the clouds of even and of morn
Float in voluptuous fleeces o'er the hills;
Let the red wine within the goblet boil,
Cold as a bubbling well; let faint-lipp'd shells,
On sands, or in great deeps, vermilion turn 20
Through all their labyrinths; and let the maid
Blush keenly, as with some warm kiss surpris'd.
Chief isle of the embowered Cyclades,
Rejoice, O Delos, with thine olives green,
And poplars, and lawn-shading palms, and beech, 25
In which the Zephyr breathes the loudest song,
And hazels thick, dark-stemm'd beneath the shade:
Apollo is once more the golden theme!
Where was he, when the Giant of the Sun
Stood bright, amid the sorrow of his peers? 30
Together had he left his mother fair
And his twin-sister sleeping in their bower,
And in the morning twilight wandered forth
Beside the osiers of a rivulet,
Full ankle-deep in lilies of the vale. 35
The nightingale had ceas'd, and a few stars
Were lingering in the heavens, while the thrush
Began calm-throated. Throughout all the isle
There was no covert, no retired cave
Unhaunted by the murmurous noise of waves, 40
Though scarcely heard in many a green recess.
He listen'd, and he wept, and his bright tears
Went trickling down the golden bow he held.
Thus with half-shut suffused eyes he stood,
While from beneath some cumbrous boughs hard by 45
With solemn step an awful Goddess came,
And there was purport in her looks for him,

Which he with eager guess began to read
Perplex'd, the while melodiously he said:
'How cam'st thou over the unfooted sea?   50
'Or hath that antique mien and robed form
'Mov'd in these vales invisible till now?
'Sure I have heard those vestments sweeping o'er
'The fallen leaves, when I have sat alone
'In cool mid-forest. Surely I have traced   55
'The rustle of those ample skirts about
'These grassy solitudes, and seen the flowers
'Lift up their heads, as still the whisper pass'd.
'Goddess! I have beheld those eyes before,
'And their eternal calm, and all that face,   60
'Or I have dream'd.'—'Yes,' said the supreme shape,
'Thou hast dream'd of me; and awaking up
'Didst find a lyre all golden by thy side,
'Whose strings touch'd by thy fingers, all the vast
'Unwearied ear of the whole universe   65
'Listen'd in pain and pleasure at the birth
'Of such new tuneful wonder. Is't not strange
'That thou shouldst weep, so gifted? Tell me, youth,
'What sorrow thou canst feel; for I am sad
'When thou dost shed a tear: explain thy griefs   70
'To one who in this lonely isle hath been
'The watcher of thy sleep and hours of life,
'From the young day when first thy infant hand
'Pluck'd witless the weak flowers, till thine arm
'Could bend that bow heroic to all times.   75
'Show thy heart's secret to an ancient Power
'Who hath forsaken old and sacred thrones
'For prophecies of thee, and for the sake
'Of loveliness new born.'—Apollo then,
With sudden scrutiny and gloomless eyes,   80
Thus answer'd, while his white melodious throat
Throbb'd with the syllables.—'Mnemosyne!
'Thy name is on my tongue, I know not how;

'Why should I tell thee what thou so well seest?
'Why should I strive to show what from thy lips   85
'Would come no mystery? For me, dark, dark,
'And painful vile oblivion seals my eyes:
'I strive to search wherefore I am so sad,
'Until a melancholy numbs my limbs;
'And then upon the grass I sit, and moan,   90
'Like one who once had wings.—O why should I
'Feel curs'd and thwarted, when the liegeless air
'Yields to my step aspirant? why should I
'Spurn the green turf as hateful to my feet?
'Goddess benign, point forth some unknown thing: 95
'Are there not other regions than this isle?
'What are the stars? There is the sun, the sun!
'And the most patient brilliance of the moon!
'And stars by thousands! Point me out the way
'To any one particular beauteous star,   100
'And I will flit into it with my lyre,
'And make its silvery splendour pant with bliss.
'I have heard the cloudy thunder: Where is power?
'Whose hand, whose essence, what divinity
'Makes this alarum in the elements,   105
'While I here idle listen on the shores
'In fearless yet in aching ignorance?
'O tell me, lonely Goddess, by thy harp,
'That waileth every morn and eventide,
'Tell me why thus I rave, about these groves!   110
'Mute thou remainest—Mute! yet I can read
'A wondrous lesson in thy silent face:
'Knowledge enormous makes a God of me.
'Names, deeds, gray legends, dire events, rebellions,
'Majesties, sovran voices, agonies,   115
'Creations and destroyings, all at once
'Pour into the wide hollows of my brain,
'And deify me, as if some blithe wine
'Or bright elixir peerless I had drunk,

'And so become immortal.'—Thus the God,   120
While his enkindled eyes, with level glance
Beneath his white soft temples, stedfast kept
Trembling with light upon Mnemosyne.
Soon wild commotions shook him, and made flush
All the immortal fairness of his limbs;   125
Most like the struggle at the gate of death;
Or liker still to one who should take leave
Of pale immortal death, and with a pang
As hot as death's is chill, with fierce convulse
Die into life: so young Apollo anguish'd: 130
His very hair, his golden tresses famed
Kept undulation round his eager neck.
During the pain Mnemosyne upheld
Her arms as one who prophesied.—At length
Apollo shriek'd;—and lo! from all his limbs   135
Celestial   *   *   *   *   *   *
        *   *   *   *   *   *   *

THE END

116

APPENDIX

THE FALL OF HYPERION

A DREAM

CANTO I

FANATICS have their dreams, wherewith they weave
A paradise for a sect; the savage too
From forth the loftiest fashion of his sleep
Guesses at Heaven: pity these have not
Trac'd upon vellum or wild Indian leaf   5
The shadows of melodious utterance.
But bare of laurel they live, dream and die;
For Poesy alone can tell her dreams,
With the fine spell of words alone can save
Imagination from the sable charm   10
And dumb enchantment. Who alive can say
'Thou art no Poet; mayst not tell thy dreams'?
Since every man whose soul is not a clod
Hath visions, and would speak, if he had lov'd
And been well nurtured in his mother tongue.   15
Whether the dream now purposed to rehearse
Be Poet's or Fanatic's will be known
When this warm scribe my hand is in the grave.

Methought I stood where trees of every clime,
Palm, myrtle, oak, and sycamore, and beech,   20
With plantane, and spice blossoms, made a screen;
In neighbourhood of fountains, by the noise
Soft-showering in mine ears; and, by the touch
Of scent, not far from roses. Turning round,

I saw an arbour with a drooping roof   25
Of trellis vines, and bells, and larger blooms,
Like floral censers swinging light in air;
Before its wreathed doorway, on a mound
Of moss, was spread a feast of summer fruits,
Which nearer seen, seem'd refuse of a meal   30
By Angel tasted, or our Mother Eve;
For empty shells were scattered on the grass,
And grape stalks but half bare, and remnants more,
Sweet smelling, whose pure kinds I could not know.
Still was more plenty than the fabled horn   35
Thrice emptied could pour forth, at banqueting
For Proserpine return'd to her own fields,
Where the white heifers low. And appetite
More yearning than on earth I ever felt
Growing within, I ate deliciously;   40
And, after not long, thirsted, for thereby
Stood a cool vessel of transparent juice,
Sipp'd by the wander'd bee, the which I took,
And, pledging all the mortals of the world,
And all the dead whose names are in our lips,   45
Drank. That full draught is parent of my theme.
No Asian poppy, nor elixir fine
Of the soon fading jealous Caliphat;
No poison gender'd in close monkish cell
To thin the scarlet conclave of old men,   50
Could so have rapt unwilling life away.
Amongst the fragrant husks and berries crush'd,
Upon the grass I struggled hard against
The domineering potion; but in vain:
The cloudy swoon came on, and down I sunk   55
Like a Silenus on an antique vase.
How long I slumber'd 'tis a chance to guess.
When sense of life return'd, I started up
As if with wings; but the fair trees were gone,
The mossy mound and arbour were no more;   60

I look'd around upon the carved sides
Of an old sanctuary with roof august,
Builded so high, it seem'd that filmed clouds
Might spread beneath, as o'er the stars of heaven;
So old the place was, I remembered none   65
The like upon the earth: what I had seen
Of grey cathedrals, buttress'd walls, rent towers,
The superannuations of sunk realms,
Or Nature's Rocks toil'd hard in waves and winds,
Seem'd but the faulture of decrepit things   70
To that eternal domed monument.
Upon the marble at my feet there lay
Store of strange vessels, and large draperies,
Which needs had been of dyed asbestos wove,
Or in that place the moth could not corrupt,   75
So white the linen; so, in some, distinct
Ran imageries from a sombre loom.
All in a mingled heap confus'd there lay
Robes, golden tongs, censer, and chafing dish,
Girdles, and chains, and holy jewelries.   80

   Turning from these with awe, once more I rais'd
My eyes to fathom the space every way;
The embossed roof, the silent massy range
Of columns north and south, ending in mist
Of nothing; then to eastward, where black gates 85
Were shut against the sunrise evermore.
Then to the west I look'd, and saw far off
An image, huge of feature as a cloud,
At level of whose feet an altar slept,
To be approach'd on either side by steps,   90
And marble balustrade, and patient travail
To count with toil the innumerable degrees.
Towards the altar sober-pac'd I went,
Repressing haste, as too unholy there;
And, coming nearer, saw beside the shrine   95

One minist'ring; and there arose a flame.
When in mid-May the sickening East Wind
Shifts sudden to the south, the small warm rain
Melts out the frozen incense from all flowers,
And fills the air with so much pleasant health   100
That even the dying man forgets his shroud;
Even so that lofty sacrificial fire,
Sending forth Maian incense, spread around
Forgetfulness of everything but bliss,
And clouded all the altar with soft smoke,   105
From whose white fragrant curtains thus I heard
Language pronounc'd. 'If thou canst not ascend
'These steps, die on that marble where thou art.
'Thy flesh, near cousin to the common dust,
'Will parch for lack of nutriment—thy bones   110
'Will wither in few years, and vanish so
'That not the quickest eye could find a grain
'Of what thou now art on that pavement cold.
'The sands of thy short life are spent this hour,
'And no hand in the universe can turn   115
'Thy hour glass, if these gummed leaves be burnt
'Ere thou canst mount up these immortal steps.'
I heard, I look'd: two senses both at once
So fine, so subtle, felt the tyranny
Of that fierce threat, and the hard task proposed.   120
Prodigious seem'd the toil, the leaves were yet
Burning,—when suddenly a palsied chill
Struck from the paved level up my limbs,
And was ascending quick to put cold grasp
Upon those streams that pulse beside the throat: 125
I shriek'd; and the sharp anguish of my shriek
Stung my own ears—I strove hard to escape
The numbness; strove to gain the lowest step.
Slow, heavy, deadly was my pace: the cold
Grew stifling, suffocating, at the heart;   130
And when I clasp'd my hands I felt them not.

One minute before death, my iced foot touch'd
The lowest stair; and as it touch'd, life seem'd
To pour in at the toes: I mounted up,
As once fair angels on a ladder flew   135
From the green turf to heaven.—'Holy Power,'
Cried I, approaching near the horned shrine,
'What am I that should so be sav'd from death?
'What am I that another death come not
'To choak my utterance sacrilegious here?'   140
Then said the veiled shadow—'Thou hast felt
'What 'tis to die and live again before
'Thy fated hour. That thou hadst power to do so
'Is thy own safety; thou hast dated on
'Thy doom.' 'High Prophetess,' said I, 'purge off   145
'Benign, if so it please thee, my mind's film—'
'None can usurp this height,' returned that shade,
'But those to whom the miseries of the world
'Are misery, and will not let them rest.
'All else who find a haven in the world,   150
'Where they may thoughtless sleep away their days,
'If by a chance into this fane they come,
'Rot on the pavement where thou rotted'st half.—'
'Are there not thousands in the world,' said I,
Encourag'd by the sooth voice of the shade,   155
'Who love their fellows even to the death;
'Who feel the giant agony of the world;
'And more, like slaves to poor humanity,
'Labour for mortal good? I sure should see
'Other men here: but I am here alone.'   160
'They whom thou spak'st of are no vision'ries,'
Rejoin'd that voice—'they are no dreamers weak,
'They seek no wonder but the human face;
'No music but a happy-noted voice—
'They come not here, they have no thought to come—   165
'And thou art here, for thou art less than they—
'What benefit canst thou do, or all thy tribe,

'To the great world? Thou art a dreaming thing;
'A fever of thyself—think of the Earth;
'What bliss even in hope is there for thee?   170
'What haven? every creature hath its home;
'Every sole man hath days of joy and pain,
'Whether his labours be sublime or low—
'The pain alone; the joy alone; distinct:
'Only the dreamer venoms all his days,   175
'Bearing more woe than all his sins deserve.
'Therefore, that happiness be somewhat shar'd,
'Such things as thou art are admitted oft
'Into like gardens thou didst pass erewhile,
'And suffer'd in these temples; for that cause   180
'Thou standest safe beneath this statue's knees.'
'That I am favored for unworthiness,
'By such propitious parley medicin'd
'In sickness not ignoble, I rejoice,
'Aye, and could weep for love of such award.'   185
So answer'd I, continuing, 'If it please,
'Majestic shadow, tell me: sure not all
'Those melodies sung into the world's ear
'Are useless: sure a poet is a sage;
'A humanist, physician to all men.   190
'That I am none I feel, as vultures feel
'They are no birds when eagles are abroad.
'What am I then? Thou spakest of my tribe:
'What tribe?'—The tall shade veil'd in drooping white
Then spake, so much more earnest, that the breath   195
Mov'd the thin linen folds that drooping hung
About a golden censer from the hand
Pendent.—'Art thou not of the dreamer tribe?
'The poet and the dreamer are distinct,
'Diverse, sheer opposite, antipodes.   200
'The one pours out a balm upon the world,
'The other vexes it,' Then shouted I
Spite of myself, and with a Pythia's spleen,

'Apollo! faded, farflown Apollo!
'Where is thy misty pestilence to creep   205
'Into the dwellings, thro' the door crannies,
'Of all mock lyrists, large self-worshipers,
'And careless Hectorers in proud bad verse.
'Tho' I breathe death with them it will be life
'To see them sprawl before me into graves.   210
'Majestic shadow, tell me where I am,
'Whose altar this; for whom this incense curls;
'What Image this, whose face I cannot see,
'For the broad marble knees; and who thou art,
'Of accent feminine, so courteous.'   215
Then the tall shade, in drooping linens veil'd,
Spake out, so much more earnest, that her breath
Stirr'd the thin folds of gauze that drooping hung
About a golden censer from her hand
Pendent; and by her voice I knew she shed   220
Long-treasured tears. 'This temple sad and lone
'Is all spar'd from the thunder of a war
'Foughten long since by giant hierarchy
'Against rebellion: this old image here,
'Whose carved features wrinkled as he fell,   225
'Is Saturn's; I, Moneta, left supreme
'Sole priestess of his desolation.'—
I had no words to answer; for my tongue,
Useless, could find about its roofed home
No syllable of a fit majesty   230
To make rejoinder to Moneta's mourn.
There was a silence while the altar's blaze
Was fainting for sweet food: I look'd thereon,
And on the paved floor, where nigh were pil'd
Faggots of cinnamon, and many heaps   235
Of other crisped spicewood—then again
I look'd upon the altar and its horns
Whiten'd with ashes, and its lang'rous flame,
And then upon the offerings again;

And so by turns—till sad Moneta cried,   240
'The sacrifice is done, but not the less,
'Will I be kind to thee for thy goodwill.
'My power, which to me is still a curse,
'Shall be to thee a wonder; for the scenes
'Still swooning vivid through my globed brain   245
'With an electral changing misery
'Thou shalt with those dull mortal eyes behold,
'Free from all pain, if wonder pain thee not.'
As near as an immortal's sphered words
Could to a mother's soften, were these last: 250
But yet I had a terror of her robes,
And chiefly of the veils, that from her brow
Hung pale, and curtain'd her in mysteries
That made my heart too small to hold its blood.
This saw that Goddess, and with sacred hand   255
Parted the veils. Then saw I a wan face,
Not pin'd by human sorrows, but bright blanch'd
By an immortal sickness which kills not;
It works a constant change, which happy death
Can put no end to; deathwards progressing   260
To no death was that visage; it had pass'd
The lily and the snow; and beyond these
I must not think now, though I saw that face—
But for her eyes I should have fled away.
They held me back, with a benignant light,   265
Soft-mitigated by divinest lids
Half closed, and visionless entire they seem'd
Of all external things—they saw me not,
But in blank splendor beam'd like the mild moon,
Who comforts those she sees not, who knows not   270
What eyes are upward cast. As I had found
A grain of gold upon a mountain's side,
And twing'd with avarice strain'd out my eyes
To search its sullen entrails rich with ore,
So at the view of sad Moneta's brow,   275

I ached to see what things the hollow brain
Behind enwombed: what high tragedy
In the dark secret chambers of her skull
Was acting, that could give so dread a stress
To her cold lips, and fill with such a light   280
Her planetary eyes; and touch her voice
With such a sorrow—'Shade of Memory!'
Cried I, with act adorant at her feet,
'By all the gloom hung round thy fallen house,
'By this last temple, by the golden age,   285
'By great Apollo, thy dear foster child,
'And by thyself, forlorn divinity,
'The pale Omega of a wither'd race,
'Let me behold, according as thou said'st,
'What in thy brain so ferments to and fro.'—   290
No sooner had this conjuration pass'd
My devout lips; than side by side we stood
(Like a stunt bramble by a solemn Pine)
Deep in the shady sadness of a vale,
Far sunken from the healthy breath of morn,   295
Far from the fiery noon and eve's one star.
Onward I look'd beneath the gloomy boughs,
And saw, what first I thought an image huge,
Like to the image pedestal'd so high
In Saturn's Temple. Then Moneta's voice   300
Came brief upon mine ear,—'So Saturn sat
'When he had lost his realms.'—Whereon there grew
A power within me of enormous ken,
To see as a God sees, and take the depth
Of things as nimbly as the outward eye   305
Can size and shape pervade. The lofty theme
At those few words hung vast before my mind,
With half unravel'd web. I set myself
Upon an eagle's watch, that I might see,
And seeing ne'er forget. No stir of life   310
Was in this shrouded vale, not so much air

As in the zoning of a summer's day
Robs not one light seed from the feather'd grass,
But where the dead leaf fell there did it rest.
A stream went voiceless by, still deaden'd more   315
By reason of the fallen divinity
Spreading more shade: the Naiad 'mid her reeds
Press'd her cold finger closer to her lips.
Along the margin sand large footmarks went
No farther than to where old Saturn's feet   320
Had rested, and there slept, how long a sleep!
Degraded, cold, upon the sodden ground
His old right hand lay nerveless, listless, dead,
Unsceptred; and his realmless eyes were clos'd,
While his bow'd head seem'd listening to the Earth, 325
His antient mother, for some comfort yet.

It seem'd no force could wake him from his place;
But there came one who with a kindred hand
Touch'd his wide shoulders, after bending low
With reverence, though to one who knew it not.   330
Then came the griev'd voice of Mnemosyne,
And griev'd I hearken'd. 'That divinity
'Whom thou saw'st step from yon forlornest wood,
'And with slow pace approach our fallen King,
'Is Thea, softest-natur'd of our Brood.'   335
I mark'd the goddess in fair statuary
Surpassing wan Moneta by the head,
And in her sorrow nearer woman's tears.
There was a listening fear in her regard,
As if calamity had but begun;   340
As if the vanward clouds of evil days
Had spent their malice, and the sullen rear
Was with its stored thunder labouring up.
One hand she press'd upon that aching spot
Where beats the human heart; as if just there   345
Though an immortal, she felt cruel pain;

The other upon Saturn's bended neck
She laid, and to the level of his hollow ear
Leaning, with parted lips, some words she spoke
In solemn tenor and deep organ tune;   350
Some mourning words, which in our feeble tongue
Would come in this-like accenting; how frail
To that large utterance of the early gods!—
'Saturn! look up—and for what, poor lost king?
'I have no comfort for thee, no—not one;   355
'I cannot cry, *Wherefore thus sleepest thou:*
'For heaven is parted from thee, and the earth
'Knows thee not, so afflicted, for a God;
'The ocean too, with all its solemn noise,
'Has from thy sceptre pass'd; and all the air   360
'Is emptied of thine hoary majesty.
'Thy thunder, captious at the new command,
'Rumbles reluctant o'er our fallen house;
'And thy sharp lightning in unpracticed hands
'Scorches and burns our once serene domain.   365
'With such remorseless speed still come new woes
'That unbelief has not a space to breathe.
'Saturn, sleep on: Me thoughtless, why should I
'Thus violate thy slumbrous solitude?
'Why should I ope thy melancholy eyes?   370
'Saturn, sleep on, while at thy feet I weep.'—

   As when, upon a tranced summer-night,
Forests, branch-charmed by the earnest stars,
Dream, and so dream all night, without a noise,
Save from one gradual solitary gust,   375
Swelling upon the silence; dying off;
As if the ebbing air had but one wave;
So came these words, and went; the while in tears
She press'd her fair large forehead to the earth,
Just where her fallen hair might spread in curls,   380
A soft and silken mat for Saturn's feet.

Long, long, those two were postured motionless,
Like sculpture builded up upon the grave
Of their own power. A long awful time
I look'd upon them; still they were the same;   385
The frozen God still bending to the earth,
And the sad Goddess weeping at his feet,
Moneta silent. Without stay or prop
But my own weak mortality, I bore
The load of this eternal quietude,   390
The unchanging gloom, and the three fixed shapes
Ponderous upon my senses a whole moon.
For by my burning brain I measured sure
Her silver seasons shedded on the night,
And ever day by day methought I grew   395
More gaunt and ghostly—Oftentimes I pray'd
Intense, that Death would take me from the vale
And all its burthens—Gasping with despair
Of change, hour after hour I curs'd myself:
Until old Saturn rais'd his faded eyes,   400
And look'd around and saw his kingdom gone,
And all the gloom and sorrow of the place,
And that fair kneeling Goddess at his feet.
As the moist scent of flowers, and grass, and leaves
Fills forest dells with a pervading air,   405
Known to the woodland nostril, so the words
Of Saturn fill'd the mossy glooms around,
Even to the hollows of time-eaten oaks,
And to the winding in the foxes' holes,
With sad low tones, while thus he spake, and sent   410
Strange musings to the solitary Pan.
'Moan, brethren, moan; for we are swallow'd up
'And buried from all godlike exercise
'Of influence benign on planets pale,
'And peaceful sway above man's harvesting,   415
'And all those acts which Deity supreme
'Doth ease its heart of love in. Moan and wail.

'Moan, brethren, moan; for lo! the rebel spheres
'Spin round, the stars their antient courses keep,
'Clouds still with shadowy moisture haunt the earth, 420
'Still suck their fill of light from sun and moon,
'Still buds the tree, and still the sea-shores murmur.
'There is no death in all the universe
'No smell of death—there shall be death—moan,
    moan,
'Moan, Cybele, moan, for thy pernicious babes   425
'Have chang'd a God into a shaking palsy.
'Moan, brethren, moan, for I have no strength left,
'Weak as the reed—weak—feeble as my voice—
'O, O, the pain, the pain of feebleness.
'Moan, moan; for still I thaw—or give me help: 430
'Throw down those Imps, and give me victory.
'Let me hear other groans; and trumpets blown
'Of triumph calm, and hymns of festival
'From the gold peaks of heaven's high piled clouds;
'Voices of soft proclaim, and silver stir   435
'Of strings in hollow shells; and let there be
'Beautiful things made new, for the surprize
'Of the sky-children'—So he feebly ceas'd,
With such a poor and sickly sounding pause,
Methought I heard some old man of the earth   440
Bewailing earthly loss; nor could my eyes
And ears act with that pleasant unison of sense
Which marries sweet sound with the grace of form,
And dolourous accent from a tragic harp
With large-limb'd visions. More I scrutinized: 445
Still fix'd he sat beneath the sable trees,
Whose arms spread straggling in wild serpent forms,
With leaves all hush'd: his awful presence there
(Now all was silent) gave a deadly lie
To what I erewhile heard: only his lips   450
Trembled amid the white curls of his beard.
They told the truth, though, round, the snowy locks

Hung nobly, as upon the face of heaven
A midday fleece of clouds. Thea arose,
And stretch'd her white arm through the hollow dark, 455
Pointing some whither: whereat he too rose
Like a vast giant seen by men at sea
To grow pale from the waves at dull midnight.
They melted from my sight into the woods:
Ere I could turn, Moneta cried—'These twain   460
'Are speeding to the families of grief,
'Where roof'd in by black rocks they wait in pain
'And darkness for no hope.'—And she spake on,
As ye may read who can unwearied pass
Onward from the Antichamber of this dream,   465
Where even at the open doors awhile
I must delay, and glean my memory
Of her high phrase:—perhaps no further dare.

CANTO II

'MORTAL, that thou mayst understand aright,
'I humanize my sayings to thine ear,
'Making comparisons of earthly things;
'Or thou might'st better listen to the wind,
'Whose language is to thee a barren noise,   5
'Though it blows legend-laden through the trees—
'In melancholy realms big tears are shed,
'More sorrow like to this, and suchlike woe,
'Too huge for mortal tongue, or pen of scribe.
'The Titans fierce, self-hid, or prison-bound,   10
'Groan for the old allegiance once more,
'Listening in their doom for Saturn's voice.
'But one of our whole eagle-brood still keeps
'His sov'reignty, and rule, and majesty;
'Blazing Hyperion on his orbed fire   15

'Still sits, still snuffs the incense teeming up
'From man to the sun's God: yet unsecure,
'For as upon the Earth dire prodigies
'Fright and perplex, so also shudders he:
'Nor at dog's howl, or gloom-bird's Even screech,   20
'Or the familiar visitings of one
'Upon the first toll of his passing bell:
'But horrors, portion'd to a giant nerve,
'Make great Hyperion ache. His palace bright,
'Bastion'd with pyramids of glowing gold,   25
'And touch'd with shade of bronzed obelisks,
'Glares a blood red through all the thousand courts,
'Arches, and domes, and fiery galeries;
'And all its curtains of Aurorian clouds
'Flush angerly: when he would taste the wreaths   30
'Of incense breath'd aloft from sacred hills,
'Instead of sweets, his ample palate takes
'Savour of poisonous brass and metals sick.
'Wherefore when harbour'd in the sleepy West,
'After the full completion of fair day,   35
'For rest divine upon exalted couch
'And slumber in the arms of melody,
'He paces through the pleasant hours of ease,
'With strides colossal, on from hall to hall;
'While, far within each aisle and deep recess,   40
'His winged minions in close clusters stand
'Amaz'd, and full of fear; like anxious men
'Who on a wide plain gather in sad troops,
'When earthquakes jar their battlements and towers.
'Even now, while Saturn, rous'd from icy trance   45
'Goes, step for step, with Thea from yon woods,
'Hyperion, leaving twilight in the rear,
'Is sloping to the threshold of the west.—
'Thither we tend.'—Now in clear light I stood,
Reliev'd from the dusk vale. Mnemosyne   50
Was sitting on a square edg'd polish'd stone,

That in its lucid depth reflected pure
Her priestess-garments. My quick eyes ran on
From stately nave to nave, from vault to vault,
Thro' bowers of fragrant and enwreathed light,   55
And diamond paved lustrous long arcades.
Anon rush'd by the bright Hyperion;
His flaming robes stream'd out beyond his heels,
And gave a roar, as if of earthly fire,
That scar'd away the meek ethereal hours   60
And made their dove-wings tremble: on he flared

*   *   *   *   *   *   *   *

Notes

Keats took the narrative of incidents for this poem from Burton's *Anatomy of Melancholy* (see the passage printed at the end of the poem, p.39), and adopted his metrical form (heroic couplets) from Dryden. Part I of the poem was written in early July 1819 at Shanklin on the Isle of Wight, and Part II in early September at Winchester. Keats thought well of *Lamia*, it has pride of place in his volume, though it was one of the last poems written, and he said of it: 'I am certain there is that sort of fire in it which must take hold of people in some way—give them either pleasant or unpleasant sensation. What they want is a sensation of some sort' (*To George and Georgiana Keats*, 18 September 1819). Keats was away from Hampstead while writing *Lamia* and corresponded regularly with Fanny Brawne, with whom he was in love, and this correspondence sheds some light on the struggle of conflicting interests dealt with in the poem. Keats expresses his feelings to Fanny without restraint. Sometimes he resists the idea of being in love, sometimes is irrationally jealous and sometimes altogether abandoned to her. His emotions are of such a nature that Matthew Arnold, who admired Keats for his manly qualities, says of these letters:

> We have the tone, or rather the entire want of tone, the abandonment of all reticence and all dignity, of the merely sensuous man, of the man who 'is passion's slave'.

> (*Essays in Criticism*, 2nd series, p. 103)

Keats was, perhaps, aware of a discreditable element in his own feelings towards Fanny when he wrote *Lamia*. Lycius is depicted as a self-centred lover (II, 56-80) and his dilemma lies in having to choose between an ignoble abandonment of the world with Lamia and coldly reductive logic with Apollonius. Neither extreme repre-

18 sents a satisfactory state of mind. Keats does not rise above Lycius, however, and in his own rôle as commentator is responsible for some unpleasant lapses in the poem (for example I, 328-33).

Lamia has been extravagantly praised, as by F. T. Palgrave:

> the whole is supreme over the parts, every word in its place, and yielding its effect in fulness. The rhyme . . . is managed with an 'opulent ease', a Spenserian fluency . . . *Lamia* is truly Greek in its direct lucidity of phrase, in its touches fresh from Nature, in its descriptive details subordinated to serious human interest. It is Greek also (though of a lower phase), in its simple sensuousness . . .
>
> (*Poetical Works of Keats*, Macmillan 1884, p.274)

More moderate critics usually qualify their praise of the poem, however. Sir Sidney Colvin says:

> [in *Lamia*] thrilling vividness of narration in particular points, and the fine melodious vigour of much of the verse, have caused some students to give *Lamia* almost the first, if not the first, place among Keats's narrative poems. But surely for this it is in some parts too feverish, and in others too unequal. . . . And it has reflective passages, as that in the first book beginning, 'Let the mad poets say whate'er they please,' and the first fifteen lines of the second, where from the winning and truly poetic ease of his style at its best, Keats relapses into something too like Leigh Hunt's and his own early strain of affected ease and fireside triviality.
>
> (*Keats*, pp.168-9)

Part I

1-6. The events to be described take place before the demigods of classical lore were replaced by the fairies

resident in nature in mediaeval times. 'Dryads' are wood-
nymphs, and 'Fauns', like 'Satyrs' are half goats and
half men. Oberon, king of the fairies, wears a brooch
set with a dewdrop for a diamond (4).

7-11. Hermes is described as always falling in love (7, 80,
93). He is the messenger of the gods and so Jupiter is his
'great summoner' (11). The wording of lines 8 and 9
hints at his rôle as god of thieves, though 'stolen light'
means that he had crept lightly away.

15-16. The 'Tritons', half men and half fish, 'wither'
because they have emerged from their element. Love
renders them 'languid.' The antithesis, the rhythm of
the lines, and their compression are reminiscent of Pope,
whom Keats studied before writing *Lamia.*

19. *unknown to any Muse*: They are not to be imagined,
even by the artist or poet.

38. *tomb*: Cf. line 55.

40. Conflict, sometimes merely apparent, sometimes
actual, is characteristic of the love relationship. The
strife is 'ruddy' because it has to do with the desire of the
lips, which are flushed, and the turmoil of the heart,
which beats high.

42. *dove-footed*: Hermes wears winged sandals (cf. 23)
and a winged helmet (68). He carries the Caduceus, a
wand with two serpents twined round it.

46. *cirque-couchant*: She lies coiled in circles. Keats
coins a word with an heraldically elaborate quality in
order to express the intricacy of her shape and the rich-
ness of her colouring.

47. *gordian*: Intricate, like the knot with which Gordius
tied the yoke to the pole of his wagon. It was so artful
that only the future emperor of Asia was to be able to
untie it. Alexander cut the knot with his sword.

49. *pard*: Leopard.

50. *Eyed*: The coloured spots on a peacock's tail are
called 'eyes'.

55. *some penanced lady elf*: In fairy tales wrongdoers are
often magically closed up in an animal body as punish-
ment.

58. *Ariadne's tiar*: The crown given by Bacchus to
135

19 Ariadne and afterwards turned into a constellation.

20 63. Proserpine was seized in Sicily by Pluto and carried off to be his bride in Hades. See *The Fall of Hyperion*, I, 35-8, note, p.198.

68. *crown'd with feathers*: See line 42, note.

73. The Muses, who preside over the arts and sciences, are entertaining the gods with songs which they accompany on the lute.

75. Cf. the *Ode to Psyche*, 30, p.79. Heroic couplets are occasionally broken by an Alexandrine, a line of twelve syllables like this one. The lengthened line is suited to its sense here, as is line 300. Apollo was god of music (see *Hyperion*, III, 10-28, note, p. 193).

78. *Phœbean dart*: Phœbus is the sun god and so his 'dart' is a sunbeam.

80. *Too gentle*: See line 7, note, and cf. line 93. Keats uses 'gentle in the mediaeval sense of 'courtly'.

81. *star of Lethe*: The Roman name of Hermes is Mercury, so he is one of the planets. He conducted the souls of the dead to Hades, where the river Lethe flows.

82. *rosy eloquence*: Cf. lines 22-5.

83. *high inspired*: See line 115, note.

87. *Bright planet*: Cf. line 81.

89. *by my serpent rod*: See line 42, note.

92. *brilliance feminine*: Cf. lines 47-53.

21 98. The tendrils and branches are burdened by fruit.

103. *Silenus*: Sileni are like Satyrs but are elderly, lecherous and have horse-ears.

107. *weïrd syrops*: Syrups with supernatural qualities.

112-15. Heroic couplets are occasionally varied, as here, with a triplet.

114. *psalterian*: Perhaps because his words have the sound of a psaltery, an ancient stringed instrument. Alternatively, Keats may mean that the oath is solemn, like the words of a psalm book.

115. *Circean*: Lamia has supernatural powers, like the beautiful witch Circe who changed Odysseus's men into swine.

116. *damask*: The pink colour of the damask rose.

22 130. *Dash'd*: Daunted or abashed.

131. *printless verdure*: Human beings, who leave foot- 22
prints on the grass, do not enter these glades.

132. Lamia has 'swoon'd' with the effort of casting her
spell and Hermes is 'languid' because overcome with
desire.

133. His slender Caduceus is used as a magician's wand
would be.

141. *bland*: Coaxing.

143. *to the lees:* To the last drop.

145. Cf. *Ode on a Grecian Urn*, 25-30.

148. *besprent*: Sprinkled.

153. *train*: Her elongated body.

156. Cf. line 51.

157. As the flow of lava from a volcano destroys the
bright meadows.

158. *brede*: A band of woven fabric.

163. *rubious-argent*: Ruby-silver. The words are heraldic. 23

167. *luting soft*: Like the lute, her voice is mellifluous.
Cf. *Isabella*, 278.

173-9. Keats assumes a Miltonic manner in describing
the vicinity of Corinth on the mainland of Greece, where
Lamia now is.

182. She is filled with emotion occasioned by her escape
when she looks at her reflection in the pool.

186. *braid*: A plaited fabric in the form of a band.

188. Sat with her skirts spread round her, listening to a
minstrel.

189-99. Lamia is both innocent and experienced (Cf.
Fancy, 79-89) so that although 'unshent' (unspoiled) she
knows how to impart pleasures so subtle that only her
skill could disentangle them in that chaotic realm of sen-
sation where pain and pleasure are akin. The ideas con-
tained in these lines are so shabby that they require
their pretentious elaboration of expression in order to
be stated at all.

206. *Elysium*: The western island where the souls of 24
the virtuous enjoy happiness. Elysium is 'faint' because
inhabited by insubstantial spirits.

207-8. Beneath the sea where the sea-nymphs ('Nereids')
lived. Thetis was one of the Nereids.

24   209-10. Bacchus, god of wine, came from the East. 'Glutinous' describes the heavy gum which exudes from the pine tree.

211-12. Mulciber (Vulcan) the craftsman was thrown from heaven by Jupiter. Milton describes him as a fallen angel responsible for the architecture of hell (*Paradise Lost*, I, 730-51). 'Piazzian' from 'piazza' here refers to the colonnaded front of a building said to face the palatial gardens of Pluto, ruler of the Underworld. 'Far' describes the vista of columns.

217. Lycius lies first in the chariot-race where competitors vie with each other.

25   229. *better'd his desire*: Gave him more than he had prayed for.

235-6. Lycius's imagination is given over to metaphysical speculation which verges on the mystical, as Plato's discussion of the real and the 'shadowy' sometimes does. Cf. Keats's speculations in the *Ode on a Grecian Urn*, p.76.

248. Orpheus could not resist looking at Eurydice while rescuing her from Hades, even though he had been warned that the consequence would be the loss of her.

252. She is so bewilderingly beautiful that his senses are intoxicated.

256. *chain*: She had secured him.

259. *belie*: Arouse false expectations.

261-7. Lycius supposes that she is divine—a demigod controlling the rivers or the woods, or a star and so partly responsible for the music of the spheres.

26   275. *nice*: Discriminating. Her home, she implies, is among the demigods.

283. *essence*: The insubstantial element of which gods are made.

285. Gods have unknown appetites which are satisfied in unknown ways.

288. See lines 244-6.

293. *amenity*: Agreeableness.

27   300. See line 75, note. Just as human beings would catch their breath, the stars catch the light they emit on hearing this celestial music.

313-14. Her life had been as pleasant as wealth alone **27** could make it with no one to love.

317-21. She had seen him on the eve of the festival to Adonis but during the festival days saw no more of him, and wept because she could only 'adore' without re-quital of her love. Adonis was beloved of Venus. He was killed by a boar and taken to Elysium. He is associated with fertility rites, so the herbs gathered for his feast are 'amorous'.

323. *lays*: Songs. Her words are music to his ears.

325. *woman's lore*: Talk of love.

327: As she is human he can take simple pleasure in her.

329. *Peris*: Persian demigods of great beauty.

333. *Pyrrha*: Wife of Deucalion, the Noah of classical mythology. After the flood Deucalion and Pyrrha re-populated the earth with men and women by throwing stones behind them. Deucalion's stones became men and Pyrrha's became women.

339. *save*: That is, heal the wounds of love. **28**

347. *comprized*: Taken up in her.

352. *lewd*: Unlearned because pagan.

360. The shadows gather together beneath projections of buildings.

370. She perspires with fear. **29**

386. *Sounds Æolian*: Musical sounds produced by air being blown over strings.

394. *flitter-winged verse*: The poetic tale must go where it is guided like a weak, blind bat led on by instinct.

396-7. Lycius and Lamia are among the 'elect' (cf. II, 6) who have known what it is to love. Those who can sympathize would find it pleasant to leave them shel-tered from the interference of worldly people who can-not believe in love.

Part II

6. *non-elect*: Those whose fortune it is not to have been **30** in love.

8-9. Lycius might have afforded another proof that the generalization is false; have 'frowned' at the moral by proving that love does not always turn to bitterness. On

30 the other hand he might have given proof that it is true. Lines 1-15 are unnecessarily obscure, and Keats may mean that the moral, by 'frowning' at Lycius, asserts its truth.

11-15. Love protectively guards them from anything that may cause discord between them.

22-5. Cf. *Ode to Psyche*, 15-20.

24. *tythe*: tithe; here 'a bit'.

27. *Deafening*: Drowning out.

31. Lamia's home is purple within because the colour suggests opulence as well as passion.

31 32. *bourn*: Boundary.

34. *penetrant*: She knows his thoughts.

36. *empery*: She rules over their secluded world.

39. 'Thought' and 'passion' cannot be alive together.

48. The morning and evening star is the planet Venus, goddess of love.

49. Why do you persuade yourself that you have been deserted?

51. Love is associated with the flow of the blood (see I, 40, note) and also with pain (see I, 189-99, note).

53. *labyrinth*: Place in a labyrinth, which would baffle escape.

55. Lycius banishes her fears (or hopes to do so) by kissing her.

32 74. *Luxurious in her sorrows*: He enjoys seeing her in grief.

76. *sanguineous*: Flushed with anger.

77. He is too youthful to show such a sign of anger.

79-80. Apollo slew Python, an enormous snake that lived on Mount Parnassus. A temple was erected to him there.

94-7. For love of Lycius she has neglected the rites due to her dead parents.

33 102. *blind and blank*: The request is made without any reason being stated.

114. *pompousness*: Desire for ostentation.

115-16. She put her mind to making a magnificent occasion of a ceremony that held no joy for her.

122-3. A magical palace does not require substantial

supports. This one is charmed into existence by a super- **33**
natural music.

135. Her contentment lies in her work of creation, her **34**
discontent in the occasion that has necessitated it.

136. *Mission'd*: Gave directions to.

148. *silent-blessing fate*: Fate has brought Lycius happi-
ness to be enjoyed in a quiet way.

150-1. The vulgar stares are the result of a prying curi-
osity.

155. *demesne*: Mansion.

160. *daft*: Resisted.

185. *libbard*: Leopard. **35**

187. *Ceres' horn*: The Cornucopia, which is represented
as a horn filled with the fruits of the harvest controlled
by Ceres, goddess of agriculture.

200-1. The guests talk in Greek, which has an open, **36**
musical sound.

207. *nectarous:* Like nectar, the drink of the gods.

211. *strange*: Constrained.

212. *Elysian shades not too fair:* Ghosts of the dead are
unlikely to be pleasant to look at, but an observer under
the influence of wine might see them as beautiful.

213. The god of wine is at the height of his control.

217. *osier'd gold*: Gold wrought to resemble woven
baskets.

218. *thought*: Inclination.

220. *Might fancy-fit his brows*: Each guest might choose a
garland as he wished. Each plant had a particular signi-
ficance, and Keats goes on to choose those suitable for
his personages.

224. *willow*: Is traditionally associated with deserted
lovers.

225-7. The thyrsus or staff of Bacchus, god of wine, is
entwined with tendrils of ivy or the grape-vine.

231-8. Science (formerly called 'natural philosophy') is
seen as destructive of beauty because it concentrates on
analysis. The rainbow was seen as a thing of beauty until
it was explained as a phenomenon of refraction. Tra-
ditionally, gnomes are miners.

246. Apollonius is now seen as a snake. Cf. line 288. **37**

37   259. A witchcraft is at work that attempts to destroy what is lovely.

38   268. As their hair rises in fright.

275. *The deep-recessed vision*: The depths of her eyes.

277. *juggling*: Necromantic.

279-80. Cf. line 190.

281-6. Lycius warns Apollonius that if he continues to offend the gods they may condemn him to blindness in a lonely old age, exposed to the terrors of a bad conscience, particularly in respect of the pride he has displayed in specious reasoning, necromancy and deceit.

301. *perceant*: Piercing. The word is Spenserian.

40   ISABELLA OR, THE POT OF BASIL

The narrative outline of the poem follows fairly closely a story in prose in Boccaccio's *Decameron* (the fifth tale of the fourth day), and Keats uses a stanza form of Italian origin: *ottava rima*, eight decasyllabic lines rhymed *abababcc*. Keats adopted this metre from Edward Fairfax's translation of Tasso, *Godfrey of Bulloigne* (1600). Reynolds and Keats had proposed bringing out jointly a volume of verse based on Boccaccio's tales, and *Isabella*, most of which was written in April 1818, is the immediate outcome of their decision. Keats was always able to criticize his poems, and though his friends admired *Isabella* he expressed his own later reservations in a letter to Richard Woodhouse:

> There is too much inexperience of life, and simplicity of knowledge in it—which might do very well after one's death—but not while one is alive. There are very few would look to the reality. I intend to use more finesse with the Public. It is possible to write fine things which cannot be laugh'd at in any way. Isabella is what I should call were I a reviewer 'A weak-sided Poem' with an amusing sober-sadness about it. . . . If I may so say, in my dramatic capacity

I enter fully into the feeling: but in Propria Persona I **40**
should be apt to quiz it myself—There is no objection
of this kind to Lamia—A good deal to St. Agnes Eve
—only not so glaring . . .

(21 September 1819)

The poem was enthusiastically received by Keats's
admirers, and was very well thought of during the
nineteenth century. Charles Lamb, for instance, said
that:

The finest thing in the volume [*Poems of 1820*] is the
paraphrase of Boccaccio's story of the Pot of Basil . . .
those never-cloying stanzas which . . . should disarm
criticism, if it be not in its nature cruel; if it would not
deny to honey its sweetness, nor to roses redness, nor
light to the stars in Heaven . . . .

(*The New Times*, 19 July 1820;
Lamb's Criticism, ed. E. M. W. Tillyard, pp.108-10)

Lamb wrote in this vein because he wished to counter the
unsympathetic criticism Keats had received in *The
Quarterly Review* and *Blackwood's Edinburgh Magazine*
(in April and August 1818). Nevertheless, Lamb is
vaguely adulatory and more recent critics have been
content to praise the poem chiefly for the numerous
passages where Keats's skill is most clearly seen, such
as that in which Lorenzo's ghost speaks in querulous,
shadowy tones (stanzas XXXVIII-XLI). Robert Bridges
says:

The story is unpleasant, and is the worst executed of
the three [finished tales]; but the poet has overcome
the gruesomeness with skill—he parenthetically in-
terrupts his narration to confess the difficulty,—yet
he seldom stays for many lines together above his
weaker vein: the appearance of Lorenzo's ghost to
Isabella, from stanza XXXI onwards, being the best
sustained passage. The poem has many examples of
Keats' originality of imagination and felicity of phrase,
but is tainted throughout by a characteristic ægri-
tude [sickness] of passion, which makes the best

143

40   occasion to speak of the curiously close similarity which exists between him and the school of painting which had Rossetti for its head.

> (*Poems of John Keats*, ed. G. Thorn Drury, Lawrence & Bullen, 1896, I, lv-lvi)

M. R. Ridley makes a valuable analysis of *Isabella* in his chapter on the poem in *Keats' Craftsmanship*. The 1684 translation of the *Decameron* used by Keats is included in the chapter.

2. Lorenzo is described as a pilgrim devoted to the service of Love. Keats maintains such religious associations in the imagery of the poem.

4. *malady*: They are love-sick.

41   **21.** He would make his devotions at the time when she said her evening prayers. The phrase 'watch and pray' preserves this sense of the word 'watch'.

26. *break*: Beginning.

28. *boon*: The gift of her love.

34. *within the rose's just domain*: Where a rosy colour should naturally rule.

35-6. Isabella's beauty had never been spoiled by grief (33), but now her unfulfilled longing causes her to waste away. Keats compares her to a young woman, emaciated by her attempts to give relief to ('lull') her sick child.

39. If she is governed by love, as her looks indicate, she will share her grief with me. Keats's conceit is strained and rather ugly. Such awkward lapses are frequent, particularly in the opening stanzas. See, for instance, 34, 35-6, 40. There is some strain, also, in the unorthodox use of words such as 'break' (26), 'anguished' (49), 'shrive' (64).

40. *'twill startle off her cares*: Her surprise at my declaration of love, will cause her to forget her sorrow.

44-5. *still the ruddy tide . . . puls'd resolve away*: The rush of his blood made it difficult for him to speak. As his pulse beat higher, his determination weakened.

46. *Fever'd his high conceit*: Heated his excited imagina-

tion. 'Conceit' means 'notion' here, but it is a high **41**
aspiring one.

52. *every symbol on his forehead high*: Every expression of **42**
his noble countenance.

62. *fear*: Frighten.

64. *shrive*: To make confession. Only Isabel can remit his
'offence'.

70. Like poetry, their kiss is harmonious. Awkward con-
ceits like this one are typical of the Keats who wrote
Endymion, though not of the author of the Odes. M. R.
Ridley says of this line that, 'apart from conveying a sen-
sation of somewhat tasteless lusciousness, [it] seems to
convey as little meaning as is possible for seven English
words arranged in a grammatical clause' (*Keats'
Craftsmanship*, p.28).

78. *dart*: Cupid's arrow.   **43**

80. *joy'd*: Rejoiced.

81. *close*: Secretly.

83. *all eves*: Every evening. Keats expresses it in a
heavy-handed way, and the repetition in these lines,
which is meant to show the passage of time, is rather
clumsy.

85. *musk*: Plants with a musky odour.

88. Our 'idle ears' have the pleasure of hearing their
story in verse, but that is because of the sad conclusion.

89-104. The argument in the two stanzas is that, as
Isabella and Lorenzo enjoyed their love for one another,
there is something to set against their later unhappiness,
and we cannot regard them as altogether unfortunate.

91. *in fee*: The sighs are a tribute paid to those whom we
regard as superior because they loved well.

95. *Theseus' spouse*: Theseus's wife was Ariadne, who
saved him from the Minotaur (a monster, part human
and part bull) in the labyrinth at Crete. She sailed away
with him, but he abandoned her on the island of Naxos.
As faith was not kept, Keats makes an exception of this
love. Sacrifices were made on Crete to a bull god in very
early times, and the legend of the Minotaur originated
then. Ovid relates the story of Theseus and Ariadne in
the *Metamorphoses*, Book VIII.

43 97-8. In general, lovers are assigned a brief period of bliss that compensates for a great deal of unhappiness.

99. *Dido*: She was abandoned by Aeneas, cast herself upon a funeral pyre, and so went to the Underworld. When Aeneas spoke to her later in Hades she remained silent. Keats does not make an exception of this love story, perhaps because Aeneas left Dido by divine command, not because he wished to do so. The legend is related in Vergil's *Aeneid*, Books IV and VI.

101-2. Lorenzo is murdered and hastily buried, so his corpse is not properly prepared by embalming it with spices, such as the 'Indian clove'. The clove is 'warm' because hot on the tongue.

103-4. The bees are 'almsmen' because they are provided for by the flowers which make a gift of their honey. The statement in line 104 is made for its poetic effect rather than for its literal truth.

44 107. *swelt*: To faint with heat or to sweat.

109-10. These slaves had once been warriors who carried quivers of arrows at the hip.

111-12. Many persons worked at the extraction of alluvial gold from river sand. This involved labouring all day in the river, made 'dazzling' by the sun.

113. *Ceylon diver*: The pearl diver whose ears may be damaged by changes in pressure as he dives (115).

119. *Half-ignorant*: The brothers are only partially aware of the miseries they are responsible for. The image in the two lines that follow is of a machine which the brothers operate, but which has movements beyond their immediate knowledge. This machine has the attributes of an instrument of torture, as the words 'racks', 'pinch' and 'peel' imply.

121-8. The repetitions and antitheses which are characteristic of Keats's style in *Isabella* are very evident in this stanza. Keats may be writing in defiance of Leigh Hunt who had pronounced such devices artificial. Hunt's dislike of these 'Italian' devices is expressed in his *Critique on Fairfax's Tasso*. Compare this stanza with stanzas XI and LIII, where the repetitions have a greater significance for the development of the tale. Keats seems to give vent to some personal irritation in his **44** description of the brothers. The middle rhyme in line 127 and the colloquial 'in the name of Glory' of line 128 give the effect of a circling exasperated speech.

123. *orange-mounts*: Perhaps an ascent or series of terraces in a garden planted with orange trees.

124. *lazar stairs*: Steps where lepers came to beg.

125. *red-lin'd accounts*: Neatly ruled account books.

126. *songs of Grecian years*: Poetry handed down from ancient times.

131. *that land inspired*: Palestine.

132. The suspicious nature of the brothers is emphasized. They shield themselves behind walls (are 'paled in') in the midst of their estates ('vineyards') and they have a confused notion that all men are out to get something from them or to take advantage of them. At the end of this line Keats's manuscript has a full stop, one transcript has a dash, another a comma.

133. *The hawks of ship-mast forests*: Most of this stanza **45** is written in a laborious and obscure manner. The line might mean that the brothers are like birds of prey ('hawks') that fatten on imported merchandise which they take up at the docks (where there is a 'forest' of masts).

134. Like 'mules', the brothers always carry the load of responsibilities entailed by their wealth ('ducats') and their intrigues ('old lies'), and like mules they are too stupid to know that this is burdensome. 'Ducats' are coins.

135. They are quick to seize upon anyone they can take advantage of, such as the stranger or the spendthrift.

136. Being merchants, they had a smattering of many languages.

140. *Hot Egypt's pest*: Keats curses their sharp eyes, possibly with the infection which causes so much blindness in Egypt.

143-4. Self-preservation in the commercial sphere requires a constant and terrified watch for possible dangers.

150. *ghittern*: A stringed instrument of Boccaccio's time.

45 151-2. Keats apologizes for giving way to an indignant outburst in the preceding stanzas. Boccaccio is more restrained.

155-6. Boccaccio does not censure the brothers for their mercenary ways, though Keats has departed from the 'piteous theme' in order to do so (stanzas XIV-XVIII). Keats undertakes, in these two lines, not to deviate again from the old tale.

159. *stead*: To render service.

46 168. *his olive-trees*: His estates.

187-8. *ere the hot sun . . . eglantine*: Before the sun takes up the drops of dew as the beads of a rosary are picked up one by one.

47 195. *matin-song*: Early morning song.

209. *their murder'd man*: Lamb (in his review—see head-note) was the first of many writers to extol this anticipatory figure of speech (prolepsis). M. R. Ridley points out how this line and the last line of the stanza make it, from the dramatic point of view, the 'high water mark' of the poem:

> There is the stage set, the three figures on it, the audience expectant. We wait for the details of the crime; but Keats knew better than Boccaccio. The curtain falls; and when it rises there are only two figures and a grave.
>
> (*Keats' Craftsmanship*, p.37)

213. *Keeps head*: The fish is depicted as lying in the current where a small tributary enters a river.

48 221. Just as blood-hounds never rest until they have tracked down a murderer and flushed him from his 'covert', so the ghost of a murdered man is not at peace.

229-30. Isabella continues to hope, but she might just as well adopt the dress of a widow, and stifle her hopes, which are a torment.

236. *luxury*: Of imagination, but also the indulgent luxury of feeling sorry for herself.

243. *the golden hour*: Sunrise.

245-7. Her thoughts become less self-centred, which makes them more urgent.

251. *sick west*: The west wind. **49**

252. *roundelay*: The music of the wind, but the word is suggestive of dead leaves being swirled about.

254-5. *dares to stray . . . north cavern*: Before the wind turns to the north. In this case, before Isabel learns that Lorenzo is dead. Her present state is preparatory, just like the west wind. Later, her state is wintry (cf. 264).

262. *Hinnom's vale*: A valley into which the Jews cast refuse and the bodies of animals and criminals. Fires were kept burning to prevent infection, and the smoke from such a fire would carry the stench of corruption. It was here that Ahaz burned his children as a sacrifice to false gods.

264. *in her snowy shroud*: She is passing towards death.

268. *feather'd pall*: The ease that would be given by death.

269-72. Perhaps the Indian is attacked while asleep. Perhaps he has hypnotically induced a condition in which he is free from pain, but is recalled to his senses by an attempt at surgery.

286. *palsied Druid's harp unstrung*: Lorenzo's voice had **50** been melodious, like that of the 'soft lute' (278), but is now like an instrument with strings relaxed. The Druid who fumbles at the harp once had supernatural powers. Notice, in this stanza and those that follow, the many ways in which Keats emphasizes the dim feebleness of the ghost.

290. *phantom fear*: Fear of ghosts.

292. *unthread the horrid woof*: Lorenzo discloses what has happened. These happenings are described as threads in the fabric of past events.

303. *upon my heather-bloom*: Upon the heather that grows **51** on my grave. The forlorn and injured tone of the ghost in this stanza emphasizes his faintness.

306. *skirts*: Lorenzo's ghost cannot depart. He dwells on the outskirts of life and its sounds cause a stir of protest in him.

307. We are reminded that Lorenzo's burial was attended by no religious rites.

316. *That paleness*: Isabella's pallor.

51 317. *the bright abyss*: Heaven.

320. *essence*: The insubstantial element of which ghosts are made.

321-2. *dissolv'd, and left . . . slow turmoil*: Lorenzo's ghostly essence disappears, leaving only a disturbance of the more substantial gloom. In lines 323-6 the disturbance is compared to a visual effect sometimes experienced when the closed eyes are pressed into a pillow.

52 334. *Sweet Spirit . . . school'd my infancy*: Lorenzo's story has taken away her childish belief that events are pre-ordained (331-2). Her brothers have violently interfered with fate.

342. While she tests the truth ('inmost') of the dream.

348. *feverous hectic flame*: To the nurse it seems that Isabella's mind is deranged and she is alarmed to see her smile (350).

53 370. Isabella had embroidered the glove herself.

54 385-92. Keats is aware of the dispassionately laconic manner in which old ballads relate horrible events, a manner at variance with his own compassionate and sensuous style. The present tale is told in Boccaccio's *Decameron* without elaboration, and Keats recommends the original to our attention. Keats writes in the spirit of his own times, as reflected in the verse romances of such writers as Wordsworth, Coleridge, Crabbe and Hunt, and the congeniality of his style to the times is shown in Lamb's extravagant response to the stanzas (XLVI-LIII) Keats here apologizes for. Lamb wrote in his review of the *Poems of 1820* (see headnote): '. . .there is nothing more awfully simple in diction, more nakedly grand and moving in sentiment, in Dante, in Chaucer, or in Spenser.' Lamb commends the depth of feeling shown in the poem.

393. *Perséan sword*: The sharp sword with which Perseus cut off the head of the Gorgon—a head so frightful that the sight of it turned men to stone. Perseus avoided looking directly at the Gorgon by viewing her reflection in a shield. Isabella and the old woman must look directly at this head, and because they are weak and their knife is blunt ('dull') their grisly labour is protracted.

398. *Love impersonate*: Lorenzo, while alive, was the **54**
personification of Love. Keats implies, however, that
the dead head continues to personify Love.

409. *dews*: Perfumes extracted from the flowers.

412. *cold serpent-pipe*: The coiled pipe used to condense
perfumes after distillation.

416. *Basil*: An aromatic shrub. **55**

431. *jewel, safely casketed*: To Isabella the head is a
precious jewel.

433-48. Those apostrophic stanzas are decidedly not in
the spirit of Boccaccio, but Keats expresses no regrets,
as he does in stanzas XIX and XLIX.

436. *Lethean*: From a past life. The waters of Lethe, a
river in Hades, brought forgetfulness to souls who were
to be reborn.

437. *Spirits*: The spirits of the dead, as the following
lines indicate. The cypress is a graveyard tree.

442. *Melpomene*: The muse who inspires the tragic **56**
writer. Traditionally, the muses accompany their songs
on the lyre.

444. *mystery*: Religious mysteries are associated with a
story which has a heightened significance for the in-
itiate. Keats asks the muse to impart a comparable
solemnity to this tale.

447-8. *a palm/Cut by an Indian for its juicy balm*: The
comparison arouses conflicting responses. The detail of
the Indian seems irrelevant, though it seems right that
the young woman should be compared to a palm flowing
with sap. But under the circumstances it is surprising
that Keats should make her sound succulent, as 'juicy
balm' does. However, this is the sort of thing Keats does
throughout the poem—even when describing the most
unpleasant things he simultaneously calls up im-
pressions which, in other contexts, could be sensuously
attractive. When Lorenzo describes his grave, for in-
stance (298-310), he does so in terms of a peaceful
pastoral scene. Notice the introduction of fresh, attract-
ive elements into the imagery of lines 361-8. When
Isabel handles Lorenzo's head (402-16) the ghastliness
of the object is heightened by contrary impressions.

56 450. *Winter*: Later, Isabella is deprived, even, of her pot of basil.

451. *Baälites of pelf*: Their false god was money. Baal was a false god of the Israelites.

453. *elf*: Person. Spenser uses the word to mean 'man' in *The Faerie Queene*.

464. *her love's delay*: The grief she had shown at Lorenzo's long absence.

57 477. *guerdon*: Reward.

481-6. Cf. lines 433-40.

491. *melodious chuckle in the strings*: As she is demented, the chuckle is grotesque and the strings out of tune, however beautiful the instrument. Cf. lines 278-9, and lines 285-6.

58 503. *burthen*: The refrain to a song.

59   THE EVE OF ST. AGNES

Keats wrote this poem very rapidly in the last week of January 1819, basing it on the mediaeval tradition (mentioned in Burton's *Anatomy of Melancholy*) that on St. Agnes's Eve (20 January) girls might dream of their future husbands. At the time Keats was still attempting to finish the first *Hyperion* and for his new poem with its impassioned and picturesque qualities chose the Spenserian stanza in place of the sedately magnificent blank verse he had been working with. Later in the year Keats expressed some doubt about the success of the poem (see headnote to *Isabella*), and there is an implied reservation in a remark he made in a letter to John Taylor, his publisher: 'I wish to diffuse the colouring of St. Agnes eve throughout a Poem in which Character and Sentiment would be the figures to such drapery' (17 November 1819).

Although the poem is slighter than the Odes or the revised *Hyperion*, it has a freshness and vigour which make it one of Keats's triumphs. It is not marred, like *Isabella*, by strained diction and the occurrence of trivial conceits; it has a confident movement throughout, and it is free of the unhealthy lapses of *Lamia*. Keats **59** describes the experience of Porphyro and Madeline as taking place in a dream. In this poem the device is a successful way of indicating the ecstatic quality of their physical encounter, while respecting its privacy. Keats does not meddle with his lovers, but places them at a distance which is maintained to the end, for they leave the story while still in a state of enchantment. H. W. Garrod, in discussing the *Poems of 1820*, says:

> Of the longer pieces, the most perfect is, I think, *The Eve of St. Agnes*—more fully there than elsewhere we feel what Matthew Arnold means when he speaks of Keats' 'perfection of loveliness'. Yet even *St. Agnes Eve* must yield to the Odes. The Odes stand apart, if for no other reason, yet because in them, for the first time, Keats finds his own manner . . . that the versification of *Lamia* is fetched from Dryden, that *St. Agnes Eve* looks back to Spenser, that *Hyperion* is more Miltonic than it has any right to be . . . all this it is impossible not to feel. But in the Odes, as I say, Keats finds, he for the first time finds, his own manner.
>
> (*Keats*, pp. 64-5)

The Spenserian stanza used in *The Eve of St. Agnes* consists of eight five-foot iambic lines followed by a line of six feet (an Alexandrine). The rhyme scheme is *ababbcbcc*. This stanza, which Spencer used for his *Faerie Queene*, is disciplined and intricate, but moves smoothly onwards, and so is very suitable for poetry that is both lyrical and narrative. It was congenial to Keats who evolved a stanza form of comparable flexibility for the Odes (see headnote to *Ode to Psyche*). Sir Sidney Colvin says of the metre of *The Eve of St. Agnes* that:

> [Keats] shows as perfect a command of the Spenserian stanza, with its 'sweet-slipping movement,' as Spenser

59 himself, and as subtle a sense as his of the leisurely meditative pace imposed upon the metre by the lingering Alexandrine at the close.

(*Life of John Keats*, p. 398)

Colvin discusses, also, possible sources of the tale.

The text of *The Eve of St. Agnes* given in this volume is copied from the edition of 1820, though there is good reason to believe that Keats might have preferred a version of the poem which differs in certain respects. Keats wrote the poem in January and revised it in early September. The publishers approved the first version, but were shocked by some of Keats's emendations, which, in their opinion, rendered the poem 'unfit for ladies'. The effect of the emendations is merely to make a little more plain what the poem already implies (that Porphyro and Madeline meet sexually), but it was the less explicit version that was finally printed. It is very likely indeed that the restoration of the 'innocent' version was imposed on Keats by his publishers, and Woodhouse (who was legal and literary adviser to the publishers) has a note at the beginning of one of his transcripts of the poem which reads (in part): 'K. left it to his Publishers to adopt which [alterations] they pleased, & to revise the whole' (see *The Poetical Works of John Keats*, ed. H. W. Garrod, Oxford University Press, 1958, p. xxxviii). Jack Stillinger argues that there are five places where the text of *The Eve of St. Agnes* should be altered to give us a version of the poem which would '. . . embody the latest readings intended by the poet, including those that there is good reason to think were rejected by the publishers against the poet's wishes . . .' ('The Text of "The Eve of St. Agnes" ', *Studies in Bibliography*, ed. Fredson Bowers, University of Virginia, 1963, pp. 207-12). The five emendations suggested are: the addition of a stanza between VI and VII (after line 54), and the emendation of line 98, line 143, lines 145-7, lines 314-22. The alternative readings are all given in the notes below, and extracts from the correspondence between Richard

Woodhouse and John Taylor are quoted in the note on **59**
lines 314-22.

5. *Beadsman*: A pensioner set to pray for the souls of his
benefactors. Keats carefully creates a context for the
lovers. First we meet the Beadsman and the revellers, all
preoccupied with their habitual activities. After the
ecstatic meeting of the young couple they depart, leaving
life to go on very much as before, though in the case of
the Beadsman it is his death that follows.

8. *without a death*: At death the spirit passes heavenward
as the breath of the Beadsman seems to do. Because of
the cold, his breath, as he prays, appears as a visible
vapour, and so seems like clouds of incense.

12. *meagre*: Emaciated.

15. The rails on the tombs seem to confine the statues
of the dead, as the souls of the dead are confined in
Purgatory while awaiting Heaven.

16. The statues in their chapels are dumb, though they
assume attitudes of prayer. They seem frozen by the
cold, even though lifeless.

21. *Flatter'd*: Gratified.

22. He is near death and his thoughts are of the future
life.

28. *prelude*: An introductory piece of music. **60**

32. *pride*: Splendour.

34-6. Like the statues (14-16) these carved supporting
figures are immobile. Life in the castle, they seem to
assert, takes a fixed and purposeful form.

37. *argent*: The heraldic word for silver. The revellers
rush in, dressed in glittering apparel. Keats often uses
heraldic terms as befits the poem, especially for naming
colours. See stanza XXIV.

39-41. Keats likens the revellers to youthful romantic
notions of what they should be, perhaps to their own
notions of themselves.

44. *wing'd St. Agnes' saintly care*: St. Agnes is the patron
saint of virgins. She was martyred at the age of 13 and is
sometimes depicted with an angel behind her.

54. When Keats revised *The Eve of St. Agnes* he added a

60   stanza after VI, but this was deleted in the published
version of the poem, probably at the insistence of his
publishers. The added stanza reads:

> 'Twas said her future lord would there appear
> Offering, as sacrifice—all in the dream—
> Delicious food, even to her lips brought near,
> Viands, and wine, and fruit, and sugar'd cream,
> To touch her palate with the fine extreme
> Of relish: then soft music heard, and then
> More pleasures follow'd in a dizzy stream
> Palpable almost: then to wake again
> Warm in the virgin morn, no weeping Magdalen.

Jack Stillinger, in the article cited in the headnote, says
of this stanza:

> Once the possibility of sexual references had been
> opened, the line describing 'More pleasures . . . in a
> dizzy stream,' 'virgin morn,' and 'weeping Magdalen'
> (very likely an allusion to the deserted unwed mother
> of Book VI of *The Excursion*, who is called 'a weeping
> Magdalene' and 'a rueful Magdalene' in lines 814,
> 987) would similarly have rendered the poem, by the
> publishers' standard, 'unfit for ladies.'
>
> *(Studies in Bibliography*, p. 210)

61   56. Cf. *Ode to Psyche*: 'Nor virgin choir to make delicious
moan' (30).
58. *sweeping train*: Skirts sweeping along the floor.
61. *not cool'd by high disdain*: Not because she rebuffed
them contemptuously.
64. *danc'd*: This word refers to her light step.
67-8. *throng'd resort/Of whisperers*: The crowd of people
about her who converse intimately in the surrounding
din.
70. Because Madeline is taken in by her superstitious
('faery') notion she is deadened ('amort') to her sur-
roundings. But see lines 314-22, note.

71. On St. Agnes's day two lambs are blessed. Later **61** their fleece is shorn and woven by nuns into cloaks sent by the Pope to Archbishops.

77. Porphyro stands in the shadow cast by a buttress.

84. Porphyro's foes will literally attack his heart, which **62** is the stronghold of love, figuratively speaking. The addition of 'fev'rous' to qualify 'citadel' confuses the metaphor.

85. *barbarian hordes*: The hordes that attacked Rome—a continuation of the metaphor on the previous line.

88. *Against his lineage*: His family is at feud with Madeline's.

98. '*Mercy, Porphyro!*': Probably substituted for the manuscript version ('Mercy, Jesu!') at the request of Keats's publishers (see headnote).

105. *Gossip*: Woman friend. Like beldame (old woman) in line 90, the word is archaic.

115-17. See line 71, note. **63**

120-2. Porphyro, she says, must be capable of magic to be so bold. Witches, it was believed, could cause a sieve to hold water.

124. *conjuror*: Madeline plans to call up ('conjure') a vision—that of her future husband.

126. *mickle*: Much. An archaic word taken from Spenser.

133. *brook*: Restrain.

134. *enchantments cold*: Any vision Madeline succeeds in conjuring up cannot be the warm living thing.

138. *purple*: His blood is purple, and the colour is **64** associated with passion.

143. '*Go, go!*': Keats's manuscript version (' O Christ') was probably altered at the request of his publishers (see headnote).

145-7. Keats wrote:

'I will not harm her, by the great Saint Paul—'
Swear'th Porphyro—'O may I ne'er find grace
'When my weak voice shall unto heaven call . . . '.

The change was probably made at the request of the publishers (see headnote).

64 153. *beard*: Defy.

155. *churchyard thing*: She is almost in her grave.

158. *plaining*: Bewailing.

65 168-9. While she is rapt away in the magical world of dreams. Cf. lines 314-22, note.

170-1. Merlin was the son of a demon father, from whom came his magical powers, and a human mother, so his powers were returned on the night he died. He was infatuated with Nimue and disclosed to her his magical secrets, which she used to destroy him. Keats's lines are obscure, but they lay stress on the enchantment of the night. The night of Merlin's death was one on which lovers met in an atmosphere of magic spells and supernatural presences. Madeline and Porphyro's night is one of magic and fairies. The parallel between the two meetings cannot be pressed further, but Keats has a purpose in emphasizing the magical (see lines 314-22, note). The difficulty of these two lines is discussed by M. R. Ridley in *Keats' Craftsmanship*, pp. 135-8. There are numerous stories of Merlin, some connecting him with the Arthurian legend, and they date back to Celtic times. He is brought into Spenser's *Faerie Queene* and Malory's *Morte Darthur*.

173. *cates*: Foods. Keats helps to create the mediaeval atmosphere of the poem by using many archaic words.

174. *tambour frame*: A circular embroidery frame.

188. *covert*: Concealment.

amain: Exceedingly.

66 198. *fray'd and fled*: Frightened and having taken flight. Keats says in one of his letters that, 'there is a tendency to class women in my books with roses and sweetmeats, —they never see themselves dominant' (*To Charles Brown*, August 1820). Keats displays a worse fault than this, however, and often seems to delight in seeing women subjected (and, if possible, acquiescent at the same time), as in *Lamia*, I, 136-43; II, 81; *Fancy*, 81-9. There is no reason why Madeline should appear as she is depicted in this line, and Keats has lapsed into an unpleasant habit of thought.

202. *wide*: Unrestrained.

203. Silence is one of the 'ceremonies' (50) to be observed.   **66**

204-5. Her heart beats so high as to distress her.

205. *balmy*: Fragrant and soft.

213. *deep-damask'd*: Damask is a rich fabric woven with elaborate designs, which often appear three-dimensional because of the weave.

214. *heraldries*: Heraldic devices.

215. *emblazonings*: Heraldic devices, often represented on a shield.

216. The coat of arms (the 'shielded scutcheon') indicates that the family is royally descended.

218. *gules*: The heraldic term for red.   **67**

222-5. See line 316, note.

228. See Sir Sidney Colvin's remark on this line, pp. 212-3.

241. In a heathen land a prayer-book ('missal') would not be unclasped because it would not be used. What is holy would be virtually asleep. Cf. line 316, note.

247. If her gentle breathing should become audible in   **68** sleep.

250. Like a frightened being in a vast, dangerous place.

257. He wishes for a charm given by Morpheus, god of sleep, so that she may remain undisturbed. His fear that she might awaken is a part cause of his 'anguish' (255).

258. *clarion*: A shrill trumpet.

262. *azure-lidded sleep*: Cf. 'violets . . . sweeter than the lids of Juno's eyes' (*The Winter's Tale*, IV, iii, 120).

265. *gourd*: Melons are referred to.

266. *soother*: More soothing. The word also suggests 'smoother.'

267. Leigh Hunt writes in his *Autobiography*:

> I remember Keats reading to me, with great relish and particularity, conscious of what he had set forth, the lines describing the supper and ending with the words, 'And lucent syrups tinct with cinnamon.' Mr. Wordsworth would have said the vowels were not varied enough; but Keats knew where his vowels were *not* to be varied.
>
> (1860 edn., p. 269. Colvin, *Life of Keats*, p. 401)

68 267. *tinct*: tinged.

268. *argosy*: A merchant ship.

69 277. *eremite*: A religious recluse devoting his life to prayer.

280. *unnerved*: He is overcome, and so deprived of strength.

284. *salvers*: See lines 272-3.

285. The cloth he has spread droops to the ground.

288. *woofed*: Woven. His imaginings are rich, like the cloths and carpets of the setting.

290. *Tumultuous*: As the hand is swept across the strings of the lute the notes surge out together.

292. In April Keats wrote a ballad on this tale, which tells how a knight falls in love with a Circe-like enchantress. Provence, in the South of France, was the home of romantic song and of the romantic tradition.

296. *affrayed*: Frightened.

70 310. The eyes were 'spiritual' because in dreams it is not physical substance that is encountered (but see line 316, note). Also, the eyes were 'clear' of their present pitiful expression.

313. *complainings*: The sad notes of his song.

314-22. Keats wrote these lines as they appear here. When he revised the poem he altered them to read as they are printed below. When the *Poems of 1820* were set up in type, however, either Keats or, more probably, his publishers (see headnote) decided to restore the original version. The revised version reads:

> See while she speaks his arms encroaching slow
> Have zon'd her, heart to heart—loud, loud the dark winds blow.

> For on the midnight came a tempest fell.
> More sooth for that his close rejoinder flows
> Into her burning ear;—and still the spell
> Unbroken guards her in serene repose.
> With her wild dream he mingled as a rose
> Marryeth its odour to a violet.
> Still, still she dreams—louder the frost wind blows.

Richard Woodhouse, who was associated with the pub- 70
lishers, was disturbed by Keats's revision, and it is pro-
bable that the objections he states carried weight in
having the lines restored to their original form. In a
letter to the publisher, John Taylor, dated 20 September
1819, Woodhouse describes a conversation with Keats:

> There was another alteration, which I abused for 'a
> full hour by the *Temple* clock' . . . As the Poem was
> originally written, *we* innocent ones (ladies & myself)
> might very well have suppposed that Porphyro, when
> acquainted with Madeline's love for him, . . . set him-
> self at once to persuade her to go off with him, &
> succeeded & went [off] . . . to be married in right
> honest chaste and sober wise. But, as it is now altered,
> as soon as M. has confessed her love, P. winds by
> degrees his arm round her, presses breast to breast,
> and acts all the acts of a bona fide husband, while she
> fancies she is only playing the part of a Wife in a
> dream.

(printed in *The Keats Circle*, I. 92)

Woodhouse does not seem to judge the matter well,
however. The original version is not necessarily more
chaste, though it leaves a little more to the imagination.
Further, Madeline is not necessarily seduced while
asleep, and there is an alternative interpretation. Keats
interweaves dream, illusion and enchantment in the
poem, as in line 70 or lines 168-71, and Porphyro's entry
into Madeline's dream may simply mean that he enters
a realm of experience which, though physical enough,
seems magical to the participants. It should be added
that, in reply to Woodhouse's letter quoted above,
Taylor stated that if Keats 'would not so far concede
to my Wishes as to leave the passage as it originally
stood, I must be content to admire his Poems with some
other Imprint [under the sign of some other publishing
house] . . .' (see *The Keats Circle*, II, 97).

316. Porphyro becomes the 'spiritual' man with 'looks im-
mortal' of the previous stanza, and throughout the poem
Keats connects sexual passion with religious ecstasy. See,

70   for instance, lines 222-5, 241, 277, 337-9. The sexual encounter of Porphyro and Madeline is associated, also, with sleep, magic and the supernatural beings of Fairyland, all of which are at a remove from the every-day and give life an additional dimension. See the previous note.

    323. *alarum*: A call to action, given here in military terms because the 'alarum' might be sounded on a drum, as the sleet softly drums on the window panes.

71   325. *flaw*: A gust of wind.

    333. *unpruned*: Bedraggled.

    336. *vermeil*: Vermilion.

    337-9. Cf. line 277, and see line 316, note.

    343. The storm is magical, an extension of their 'dream'. See lines 314-22, note.

    344. *haggard*: Unfriendly.

    344. *boon*: Gift.

    346-9. The revellers are all stupefied with Rhenish wine and mead.

72   353-6. There are unknown dangers such as beset travellers in 'faery land'.

    355. *darkling*: See *Ode to a Nightingale*, 51, note, p. 165.

    358. *arras*: A hanging tapestry.

    376. *meagre*: See line 12, note.

73   ODE TO A NIGHTINGALE

This ode was most probably written in May 1819 and, according to Keats's friend Charles Brown, it was composed in two or three hours one morning in a Hampstead garden. Brown's account is given in his sketch 'Life of John Keats,' 19 March 1841 (see *The Keats Circle*, ed. H. E. Rollins, Vol. II, p. 65). For the series of odes that Keats wrote in April and May he evolved a stanza pattern that is formal but capable of modulation (see pp. 169-71 below), and this poem is probably the first result of the metrical experiment made in the *Ode to Psyche*. There is a very lively sensuous awareness shown in the poem, despite Keats's announced desire for oblivion. It may help, in interpreting this, to bear in mind that

Keats often links together a state of oblivion (or a loss **73**
of the self) and a heightened or especial sensitivity. In
The Eve of St. Agnes, for instance, which was composed
two months before, sleep is a state of enchantment, and
at the height of enjoyment Porphyro enters Madeline's
dream (see lines 314-22, note). In his letters Keats some-
times describes the experience of writing poetry as a
loss of personal identity coupled with a gain in aware-
ness of other things and persons:

> A Poet is the most unpoetical of any thing in existence;
> because he has no Identity—he is continually [in-
> forming] and filling some other Body—The Sun, the
> Moon, the Sea and Men and Women who are crea-
> tures of impulse are poetical and have about them an
> unchangeable attribute—the poet has none; no
> identity . . . When I am in a room with People if I
> ever am free from speculating on creations of my own
> brain, then not myself goes home to myself: but the
> identity of every one in the room begins so to press
> upon me that I am in a very little time annihilated.
>
> *(To Richard Woodhouse*, 27 October 1818)

T. S. Eliot expresses an idea of the poetic talent which is,
in some ways, similar to Keats's. In his essay 'Tradition
and the Individual Talent' (1919), Eliot says:

> Poetry is not a turning loose of emotion, but an escape
> from emotion; it is not the expression of personality,
> but an escape from personality. But, of course, only
> those who have personality and emotions know what
> it means to want to escape from these things.
>
> *(Selected Essays*, Faber 1934, p. 21)

In the first line of the poem Keats describes his state
as being both numb and painful, and asserts that this is
due to an opposing state of 'being too happy.' The
sombre tone of the first stanza gives way to elation in the
quick-moving lines that open the second stanza, though
the final lines describe a more subdued desire. The third
stanza is morbid, but the tone changes abruptly at the
opening of stanza four to hopeful expectation. These

73 rapid alternations between sombre thoughtfulness and elation continue throughout the poem and the changes of mood are more violent and more frequent than in the *Ode on a Grecian Urn*. The final change, where the poet is thrown back on his everyday self occurs at the same place in the two poems, however—at the end of the penultimate stanza. The word 'forlorn' in this poem, and the word 'desolate' in the other mark the point of transition. The song of the nightingale stirs Keats profoundly—emotions at the depth of his being are touched, and such emotions defy easy identification. That is partly why Keats feels himself to be moved simultaneously by a variety of feelings, some of which appear incompatible, and why his feelings fluctuate in an apparently bewildering manner. A level of feeling is being explored which the analytic mind finds strange; where it is lost among apparently familiar things.

There are excellent analyses of *The Ode to a Nightingale* by G. Wilson Knight and by F. R. Leavis (see Bibliography, p. 221).

2-3. Hemlock is a powerful sedative which leads to a painless death if too much is taken. Opiates relieve pain, and they, too, are poisonous.

4. *Lethe*: Souls waiting in Hades to be reborn drink the waters of Lethe and forget their past existence.

7. *Dryad*: A wood-nymph.

13. *Flora*: The Roman goddess of flowers.

14. Provence is in the south of France, where the Troubadours brought about a golden age of song.

16. *Hippocrene*: A fountain sacred to the muses on Mount Helicon. Poetry, like wine, excites the mind, though Keats decides on the former stimulant (31-3).

18. It is not only the mouth of the beaker which is stained but also the mouths of the drinkers in their abandon.

74 32. Bacchus, god of wine and of an ecstatic religious cult, is sometimes depicted riding in a chariot pulled by leopards.

33. *viewless*: Invisible. Poetry is conceived of as a spirit

more ethereal than the earthy Bacchus. Her joys are of a   **74**
purer order.

51. *Darkling*: Milton, writing poetry while blind, compares himself to the nightingale:

> . . . as the wakeful Bird
> Sings darkling, and in shadiest Covert hid
> Tunes her nocturnal Note.
>
> (*Paradise Lost*, III, 38-40)

'Darkling' (in the dark) is a mediaeval word, used occasionally in poetry.

60. Literally, the line means that Keats would return to   **75**
the earth by dying while the bird sings a funeral chant.
In the last stanza, however, it is the bird that is 'buried.'

61-2. The bird seems to have a continued tranquil existence in its species while men, more fiercely individual, strive destructively against each other for survival. Like the Grecian urn, the nightingale represents the existence of an enduring beauty set against man's transient life, and affording him relief by taking him beyond his 'sole self.'

64. *clown*: Peasant.

65-7. Keats refers us to the biblical story of Ruth because she, too, experienced a sense of longing.

71-2. At the height of transport in stanza 6 Keats is attracted by the idea of death, but now the return to himself is felt to be death-like.

73-4. The word 'elf' is used here to suggest that the imagination, like the elves of Fairyland, belongs to an enchanted world—the world Keats has just been transported to. But, like the elves, the imagination is mischievous, and this suggestion is reinforced by 'cheat' and 'deceiving.' In these lines Keats, now called back to 'normality,' tends to treat the fancy rather lightly, but he goes on to modify his view in the lines that follow.

79-80. In the last two lines of the poem Keats, still a little bewildered by the intensity of his experience, wonders about reality. Is it the world he has just been 'awake' to—the ecstatic world of the nightingale's song—or is it the common world he has now 'awakened' to?

75 Perhaps we are asleep when we are unaware of transcendent beauty, and awake only when we are made aware of it by such things as the nightingale's song (or the Grecian urn).

76 ODE ON A GRECIAN URN

Like the *Ode to a Nightingale*, this poem is very complex. There are no compact definitions of the terms it uses, one part illuminates another and there are subtle changes in mood. In the first line, for instance, the word 'still' must be taken in the sense of being calmly at rest, and also, in conjunction with 'unravished,' as indicating that something has not yet been accomplished. The word 'unravished' takes on meaning when read in connection with lines 17-18 or lines 25-8, and a further meaning when read with lines 44-5. The changes of mood in this poem are more gentle than those in the *Ode to a Nightingale*, the most obvious one being that between stanzas 2 and 3, both of which describe the same subject. Commentaries on the poem show considerable divergence in their interpretations, particularly in respect to the meaning and success of the last two lines. Some critics find that these lines lamely conclude the poem with a statement that is vague, despite its philosophic pretentiousness. Other writers find that these words present a fitting climax which has been carefully prepared for. The arguments on both sides are set out by J. M. Murry in his *Studies in Keats* (' "Beauty is Truth . . ." '), and re-examined by Cleanth Brooks in *The Well Wrought Urn*, pp. 139-52 (see Bibliography, p. 222). If the words of the poem require help, Keats gives some in his early letter to Benjamin Bailey, printed in the notes to *Bards of Passion and of Mirth*. There, Keats states an idea similar to that expressed by Plato in his analogy of the cave (*Republic* V)—that in our finer moments of perception we are aware of what exists in eternity, while our normal realities are mere shadows. Plato states that this heightened awareness of what truly exists is to be arrived at philosophically, by taking thought, but Keats tells

Bailey that speculation does not provide this knowledge, **76**
that it is directly perceived, and that the criterion of our
experiencing of these eternal truths is our awareness of
beauty. In the same letter Keats wrote:

> I have never yet been able to perceive how anything
> can be known for truth by consequitive reasoning—
> and yet it must be. Can it be that even the greatest
> Philosopher ever arrived at his goal without putting
> aside numerous objections. However it may be, O for
> a Life of Sensations rather than of Thoughts.
>
> (22 November 1817)

Keats's reasoning is similar to that found in the treatise
On the Sublime (probably 3rd century A.D.), traditionally
attributed to 'Longinus,' which contends that poetic
truths overwhelm us like a flash of lightning, rather than
attempt to convince us by argument. Perhaps Keats did
not have these ideas in mind when he wrote the ode, but
it is to be observed that the urn is seen as an object that
stands aloof from our ordinary experience. It should also
be observed that Keats defines its transcendence by im-
mobilizing ordinary experience at its most propitious
moment in the details of the scene he imaginatively de-
picts on the urn.

In his chapter on the poem Cleanth Brooks suggests
that the message of the final two lines is prepared for
dramatically by the poem and that we must read it in
context, without expecting it to 'compete with the scien-
tific and philosophical generalizations which dominate
our world.' Brooks says:

> [The] truth [given by the] sylvan historian is the only
> kind that we *have* to have. The names, dates, and
> special circumstances, the wealth of data—these the
> sylvan historian quietly ignores. But we shall never get
> all the facts anyway—there is no end to the accumu-
> lation of facts. Moreover, mere accumulations of facts
> —a point our own generation is only beginning to
> realize—are meaningless. The sylvan historian does
> better than that: it takes a few details and so orders

76   them that we have not only beauty but insight into essential truth. Its 'history,' in short, is a history without footnotes. It has the validity of myth—not myth as a pretty but irrelevant make-belief, an idle fancy, but myth as a valid perception into reality.

(The Well Wrought Urn, pp. 150-1)

1-10. The urn is an 'historian' because the scenes depicted on its two sides are both taken from some sequence of events (some 'legend'), and also because they tell us of the activities of men long dead. The scenes depicted are set among trees and in the countryside, so the urn is 'sylvan' (it tells of the inhabitants of the forest), and in stanza 5 it is addressed as a 'pastoral' (it portrays the life of shepherds or country folk). In legend, Arcady is the ideal region of pastoral contentment and is celebrated in poetry as such. Tempe, too, is a pleasant region of Grecian rustic peace. A 'timbrel' is a tambourine.

11-14. The musicians depicted on the urn are suggestive of music which might be heard, but are suggestive, also, of the beauty which is essential to all music and all works of art. The urn can tell a tale without using words, and it can produce music without making a sound because it communicates a quality all beautiful things have in common. Man's 'spirit' is sensitive to that quality.

77   31-40. Keats was familiar with the Elgin Marbles in the British Museum, and the scene he depicts on this side of the urn has some resemblance to the procession there represented. The 'little town' is not shown on the urn.

41. *Attic*: Attica is a district in Greece. Keats uses the word loosely for 'Grecian.'

brede: Embroidery. The urn is enriched by the design wrought on it, just as cloth may be enriched by embroidery.

44-5. *dost tease . . . eternity*: We are baffled when we attempt to conceive of the eternal because it is beyond our experience. In the same way there is a transcendental element in the beauty of the urn which we see must be there but which we cannot define. Because we cannot attain to a full understanding, the urn seems aloof

('cold' and 'silent'). Because all men can glimpse the per- **77**
fection, however, the urn is also a 'friend' (48) to suc-
cessive generations.

49. '*Beauty is truth, truth beauty*': Some editions (H. W.
Garrod's Oxford Text, for example) print this statement
without the inverted commas. Transcripts from Keats's
manuscript (which is lost) have no quotation marks, and
these were not inserted when the poem was first printed
in *The Annals of the Fine Arts* (No. XV, January 1820).
It has been argued that the addition of the inverted
commas gives us two statements—one by the urn and
then a concluding statement by Keats himself. J. M.
Murry says:

> The evidence is that Keats corrected his 1820 volume
> with care, and the presence of the inverted commas
> suggests to me that Keats thought the distinction
> between the utterance of the Urn and his own en-
> dorsement of it to be of some importance.
>
> (*Keats*, p. 321)

It is just as probable, however, that the last two lines of
the poem both contain the message of the urn, and that
the quotation marks are put in to point up the aphorism.

ODE TO PSYCHE   **78**

Keats included this ode in a letter to his brother George
on 30 April 1819, saying:

> The following Poem—the last I have written is the
> first and the only one with which I have taken even
> moderate pains. I have for the most part dash'd off
> my lines in a hurry. This I have done leisurely—I
> think it reads the more richly for it and will I hope en-
> courage me to write other things in even a more
> peaceable and healthy spirit.

Keats was certainly encouraged to 'write other things'
by the poem. During the next month he wrote three of
the four odes by which he is best known, and the *Ode to
Psyche* helped him find the stanza form in which they

78   were written. The poet had written sonnets of the Petrarchan and Shakespearean varieties, both having five feet to the line, but with a different arrangement of the rhymes, and so with different ways of producing their effects. The Petrarchan sonnet is divided into two parts, an octave rhymed *abbaabba* and a sestet of two or three rhymes variously arranged. Usually there is a change in perspective or mood between octet and sestet. The Shakespearean sonnet consists of three quatrians alternately rhymed, followed by a couplet (*ababcdcdefefgg*), and the culmination of the Shakespearean sonnet occurs in the couplet. Keats expressed dissatisfaction with the sonnet form, decided not long before writing the *Ode to Psyche* that he felt freer with the rondeau in couplets (see note on *Fancy*), and tried other forms such as the Spenserian stanza in *The Eve of St. Agnes*. Just before writing the *Ode to Psyche*, however, Keats wrote one of his most beautiful poems, *To Sleep*, and wrote it in sonnet form with one modification: there are three quatrains as in the Shakespearean sonnet, but the remaining two lines are placed before the last quatrain instead of at the end. The rhymes for these two lines are taken from the first two quatrains. The crisp effect of a terminal couplet would be inappropriate to the subject of the poem. After this experiment Keats turned to the *Ode to Psyche*, a poem which Ridley describes as 'a loosely connected series of variously reformed sonnets' (*Keats' Craftsmanship*, p. 205). The first fourteen lines, for instance, may be seen as two Shakespearean quatrains followed by a rather irregular sestet. Lines 24 to 35 may be viewed as a Shakespearean sonnet without the couplet, and with some lines shortened. The fourteen lines from 36 to 49 are arranged in a manner similar to those in *To Sleep*, and so are the next fourteen (50-63). The result of this experimentation with the sonnet was to provide Keats with a stanza form of his own which proved suitable for the *Ode to a Nightingale*, *Ode on a Grecian Urn* and *Ode to Melancholy*. These poems are based on a ten-line stanza—a Shakespearean quatrain followed by a Petrarchan sestet, the arrangement of the last three lines

in the sestet being varied. There was one further out- **78**
come. In September Keats wrote the Ode *To Autumn*
and prolonged his stanza by inserting after line 9, a line
to rhyme with it, making eleven lines in all. An examina-
tion of the poem will show how appropriate to the sub-
ject this delayed conclusion is.

Commentators on the *Ode to Psyche* have attempted to
find a symbolic meaning to the poem, and some of these
are discussed by Kenneth Allott in *John Keats, a Re-
assessment* (ed. Kenneth Muir, Liverpool University
Press, 1958, pp. 74-94). More simply, Keats's intention
may be taken to be the one he jokingly expresses in the
letter quoted above:

> You must recollect that Psyche was not embodied as a
> goddess before the time of Apuleius the Platonist who
> lived after the Augustan age, and consequently the
> Goddess was never worshipped or sacrificed to with
> any of the ancient fervour—and perhaps never thought
> of in the old religion—I am more orthodox than to let
> a heathen Goddess be so neglected.

Apuleius tells the story of Psyche in *The Golden Ass*.
Cupid, god of love, visited her by night, though she was
not allowed to behold him. Being persuaded that he is a
serpent, she attempts to view him while he is asleep,
but disturbs him and he departs in anger. She wanders
about, undergoing many hardships until Jupiter, taking
pity on her, makes her immortal, and she is reunited
with her lover.

F. R. Leavis, when discussing Keats's poetic achieve-
ment, his 'perfection attained within a limiting aestheti-
cism,' says:

> That exquisitely sure touch which refines and lightens
> Keats's voluptuousness cannot, we are convinced, go
> with spiritual vulgarity (an argument notably relevant
> to the *Ode to Psyche*, about the sensuous loveliness of
> which there is nothing oppressive, cloying or gross).
>
> (*Revaluation*, p. 265)

78 1. *numbers*: Verses.

2. *By sweet enforcement*: Keats cannot help himself, so compelling is the memory. Cf. Milton's *Lycidas*, 6.

4. *soft-conched*: Her ear is delicately whorled. One variety of conch (a sea-shell) is called Venus ear.

6. *awaken'd eyes*: This is no dream—but more is suggested. The imaginative perception is a heightening of ordinary experience, and at the conclusion of the *Ode to a Nightingale* Keats implies that his true 'awakening' was experienced while the imagination was fully engaged.

14. *Tyrian*: Purple, from the name of a dye once made at Tyre.

16. *pinions*: Wings. Both Cupid and Psyche are depicted as winged.

20. As the half-slumbering pair awaken, so will the expression of love in their eyes awaken too. Aurora is the light of dawn.

21. *The winged boy*: Cupid.

24-5. Apuleius's account of Psyche was written in the second century A.D., during the decline of paganism, so she is the last arrival among the Olympian gods, already 'fading.'

26-7. Phoebe is the virgin goddess, and her 'star' is the moon. Keats contrasts her with Vesper, the evening star, who is 'amorous' because identified with Venus, goddess of love. The full moon is 'sapphire-region'd' because that region of the sky through which it moves is faintly tinged with blue.

79 30. *virgin-choir*: The virgins attendant at pagan shrines.

34-5. Pagan deities were worshipped at 'shrines,' and also in 'groves' which were sacred to them. The priests and priestesses in attendance at such places of worship claimed to be able to foretell the future by reading portents or by speaking as the mouthpiece ('oracle') of the deity. The 'prophet' speaks by virtue of the power of the god or goddess, so though his message is an impassioned one (is 'heated') he is rapt away from ordinary life. He is 'pale' and in a dream-like state.

37. *fond believing lyre*: The hymns sung by unquestioningly faithful worshippers.

38-9. In pagan belief natural objects were inhabited by **79**
semi-divine beings.

41. *fans*: Wings.

50. *fane*: Temple.

52. *pleasant pain*: Cf. Keats's sensations in *Ode to a Nightingale*, 1-6.

57. *Dryads*: Wood-nymphs.

62-3. Cf. the rose-scented daisies in the ode *Bards of* **80**
Passion and of Mirth, 14.

66-7. Cupid is to visit her by night, as he did before she
offended him, though now there will be a torch to light
them.

FANCY   81

This poem and the next, *Bards of Passion and of Mirth*,
were written in late December 1818, eleven months after
the two poems, *Lines on the Mermaid Tavern* and *Robin
Hood*, to which they are related in style and theme. The
great Odes, written some four months later, contain
echoes of them but have more poetic depth and are
rhythmically more intricate and subtle. In writing to his
brother George, Keats said of *Fancy* and *Bards of
Passion* that:

> These are specimens of a sort of rondeau which I
> think I shall become partial to—because you have one
> idea amplified with greater ease and more delight and
> freedom than in the sonnet.
>
> (2 January 1819)

Despite this prediction, it was in fact the sonnet that
Keats so successfully modified to evolve the stanza form
of the Odes. In *Fancy*, Keats states that the imagination
can improve on experience because it brings together
pleasures that may not be enjoyed simultaneously and
the enjoyment may be prolonged. There is a higher form
of the imagination than this day-dreaming variety, one
which heightens our appreciation of realities, not fictions,
and this higher form is to be seen at work in Keats

81 when he writes *To Autumn* (see p. 88). *Fancy* should be compared with that poem.

17. *sear faggot*: A bundle of dry sticks.
21. *shoon*: An archaic word for shoes.
27. *high-commission'd*: The mind gives the fancy a warrant to fetch what is desired.
28. *vassals*: Chief among the servants of fancy would be the memory.

82 38. As wines are blended, so the fancy blends the delights of the three seasons, spring, summer and autumn.
56. The field mouse is said to be thin ('meagre') after hibernation in some secret 'cell.'

83 81. *Ceres' daughter*: The maiden Proserpine who was forcibly abducted by Pluto, god of the Underworld. See *The Fall of Hyperion*, 35-8, note.
85. Hebe was goddess of youth and cup-bearer to the gods. Keats depicts her as being acquiescent, unlike the reluctant Proserpine. A 'zone' is a girdle.
87. *kirtle*: gown.

ODE—'BARDS OF PASSION AND OF MIRTH'

Keats wrote this poem in a collection of plays by the Jacobeans Beaumont and Fletcher and so it may be read in conjunction with *Lines on the Mermaid Tavern*. It contains an echo of *Fancy*, and Keats spoke of the two poems together (see note on *Fancy*, p. 173). What is of more importance is that it may be compared with the *Ode on a Grecian Urn* in the light of an early letter written to Benjamin Bailey where Keats says:

> I am certain of nothing but of the holiness of the Heart's affections and the truth of Imagination—What the imagination seizes as Beauty must be truth—whether it existed before or not—for I have the same Idea of all our Passions as of Love they are all in their sublime, creative of essential Beauty.
>
> (22 November 1817)

Keats goes on to state that an encounter with 'essential

174

Beauty' is an anticipation of what is to be encountered   **83**
spiritually in eternity. The imagination, he says,

> is 'a Vision in the form of Youth' a Shadow of reality
> to come—and this consideration has further convinced
> me for it has come as auxiliary to another favourite
> Speculation of mine, that we shall enjoy ourselves here
> after by having what we call happiness on Earth re-
> peated in a finer tone and so repeated. . . . Imagination
> and its empyreal reflection is the same as human Life
> and its Spiritual repetition.

Keats's ideas on truth and beauty are further discussed
in the notes on the *Ode on a Grecian Urn*, pp. 166-9.

6. *spheres*: The old astronomers thought of the heavenly
bodies as moving round the earth in their respective
spheres.
8. *parle*: Discussion. The word is poetic.   **84**
11. *Elysian*: In Elysium the souls of the virtuous enjoy
happiness. See *Lines on the Mermaid Tavern*, 2, note.
12. *Dian*: Diana, the goddess of hunting and of the
moon.
14-16. Cf. *Fancy*, 37-8.
17-20. In eternity, beauty and truth are undivided (see
headnote) and so in Elysium 'truth' and 'philosophy' are
uttered musically (are 'melodious') or as poetry (in
'numbered' verse). Even the song of the nightingale
makes this divine sense, because it is beautiful. See also
the headnote to *Ode on a Grecian Urn*, p. 166.
24. The bards are 'immortalized' by their works.

LINES ON THE MERMAID TAVERN   **85**

This poem and the next, *Robin Hood*, were written al-
most a year before most of the verse in this volume. The
poems are light in tone and it does not appear to have
been Keats's intention that we should take them very
seriously. Keats had received two sonnets on Robin
Hood from his friend John Hamilton Reynolds and
wrote in reply (3 February 1818): 'In return for your

85 Dish of filberts, I have gathered a few Catkins, I hope
they'll look pretty . . . I hope you will like them—they
are at least written in the Spirit of Outlawry . . .'. With
this light-hearted introduction he wrote down the two
poems. It should be added, however, that Keats objects,
in the same letter, to the excessive solemnity and self-
importance which he finds in the verse of Wordsworth
and Hunt, and he makes it clear that *Lines on the Mermaid
Tavern* and *Robin Hood* are deliberately written in a vein
of gaiety because he wishes to oppose this solemn ten-
dency. The poems are written in the 'Spirit of Out-
lawry' because they are in defiant reaction. He says:

> We hate poetry that has a palpable design upon us—
> and if we do not agree, seems to put its hand in its
> breeches pocket. Poetry should be great and unob-
> trusive, a thing which enters into one's soul, and does
> not startle it or amaze it with itself, but with its
> subject . . . I don't mean to deny Wordsworth's gran-
> deur and Hunt's merit, but I mean to say we need not
> be teazed with grandeur and merit when we can have
> them uncontaminated and unobtrusive. Let us have
> the old Poets, and robin Hood.

2. *Elysium*: The Elysian Fields were that part of the
Underworld reserved for dead heroes and heroines in
classical myth.
4. *the Mermaid Tavern*: A London inn in Bread Street,
Cheapside, frequented by literary men in the opening
years of the seventeenth century. Beaumont addressed
Ben Jonson on the subject as follows:

> What things have we seen
> Done at the Mermaid! heard words that have been
> So nimble, and full of subtle flame,
> As if that every one from whence they came
> Had meant to put his whole wit in a jest
> And had resolved to live a fool the rest
> Of his dull life.

12. *Sup and bowse*: To drink, by the mouthful or in large 85
draughts.
16-17. The astrologer wrote down what he had observed
taking place among the stars. He wrote on vellum, made
of sheepskin, using an old-fashioned quill pen.
19. *new old-sign*: The sign of the Mermaid, one of the
constellations in the Zodiac, is as old as the heavens
themselves, though now it has been renewed in being
replaced by the sign-board from the tavern.
21. As they drink a toast to the Mermaid the poets smack
their lips in enjoyment of their wine.

ROBIN HOOD   86

The friend addressed is John Hamilton Reynolds. See
the note on the previous poem, p. 175.

10. Robin Hood and his band of men, being outlaws,
'occupied' Sherwood Forest without paying rent to any-
one.
13. *ivory*: A hunting-horn.
17. *wight*: A person, perhaps lost, depicted here as
startled by echoing laughter in the depths of the lonely
forest. The word is archaic.
21. *seven stars*: The Pleiades or the constellation of the
Great Bear.
22. *polar ray*: The light from the pole star.
30. *pasture Trent*: Pasture lands along the river Trent 87
which flows near Sherwood Forest.
33. *morris*: An old dance in costume, often representing
Robin Hood and his men.
34. *song of Gamelyn*: An anonymous mediaeval verse
romance which has much in common with the story of
Robin Hood. This tale is the ultimate source of *As You
Like It*.
36. *the 'grenè shawe'*: The green wood. Keats uses suit-
ably archaic words, and other words in the poem have an
archaic flavour. The ballad 'Robin Hood and Guy of
Gisborne,' first published in Percy's *Reliques* (1765)
commences with the lines:

87 When shaws beene sheene, and shradds [swards] full
      fayre,
    And leaves both large and longe . . .

    44. The oaks have been felled for shipbuilding.
    62. *burden*: The chorus of a song.

88   TO AUTUMN

This ode was written at Winchester in September 1819.
It is the last poem written for this volume, and in some
respects it is Keats's best piece of work. It shows re-
markable skill in the use of rhythm to amplify the
sense of the lines, in its careful accumulation of sensu-
ous effect, and in brilliant use of personification. Autumn
is presented in its full roundness, and it is to be noticed
that the feeling of the first two stanzas is modified by a
different emotion in the last. In the personification in the
second stanza, Keats does not represent Autumn con-
ventionally with a figure drawn from classical mythology
as poets so often do. Instead, Autumn is seen as four of
the persons who may be encountered at the time of har-
vest, and they are heavy with the fullness of the season
emphasized in the first stanza. The personifications are
very real and very relevant. The figure (most probably a
girl, though Autumn is traditionally masculine) who
sits on the granary floor, *is* Autumn, not a symbol of the
season. In 'winnowing,' grain with the husks threshed
off is thrown into the air so that the wind can separate
the chaff from the heavier grain. The chaff streams before
the wind, so it may be regarded as the golden hair of the
Autumn who sits in the person of a girl with her hair
'soft-lifted.' As a 'gleaner,' Autumn is given life by the
rhythm. F. R. Leavis says of lines 19-20:

In the step from the rime-word 'keep,' across (so to
speak) the pause enforced by the line-division, to
'Steady' the balancing movement of the gleaner is
enacted.

                                    (*Revaluation*, pp. 263-4)

In the last stanza Keats's picture is more bleak, his **88** sounds muted and the colours faded. Autumn is a passing away as well as a fruition, and in some of the words of the stanza death is hinted at.

18. *swath*: The width of corn cut by a mower's sickle.
26. *stubble-plains*: Now that it is autumn the harvest is in, leaving the fields bare except for the sharp stubble.
28. *sallows*: Low-growing willows. Garrod emends the **89** word to 'shallows.'

ODE ON MELANCHOLY

This is probably the last of the odes written in April and May 1819. Keats had been reading Burton's *Anatomy of Melancholy*, and in the first stanza he cites the symbols conventionally associated with melancholy before going on to say that the emotion is most acutely felt in the presence of beautiful things. This is partly because beauty and the enjoyment of beauty are transient; a discovery that is made, also, in the *Ode to a Nightingale* and the *Ode on a Grecian Urn*. In those poems Keats's hold on beauty is precarious. The ecstasy he feels in the nightingale's song, and the quieter pleasure he enjoys when regarding the perfection of the urn, both slip away in the last stanzas of the poems, and the transience of beauty is proved by the experience described. The *Ode on Melancholy* makes a more dogmatic statement on impermanence.

Keats cancelled his original first stanza to the poem, perhaps because its macabre and melodramatic tone is at variance with the full-bodied, sometimes voluptuous, quality of the remaining stanzas. The deleted stanza reads:

Though you should build a bark of dead men's bones,
  And rear a phantom gibbet for a mast,
Stitch shrouds together for a sail, with groans
  To fill it out, blood-stained and aghast;
Although your rudder be a dragon's tail
  Long sever'd, yet still hard with agony,

89   Your cordage large uprootings from the skull
       Of bald Medusa, certes you would fail
          To find the Melancholy—whether she
             Dreameth in any Isle of Lethe dull.

William Empson says of the poem that:

> The perfection of form, the immediacy of statement,
> of the Ode, lie in the fact that . . . [opposite notions]
> are all collected into the single antithesis which unites
> Melancholy to Joy. Biographers who attempt to show
> from Keats's life how he came by these notions are
> excellently employed, but it is no use calling them in
> to explain why the poem is so universally intelligible
> and admired; evidently these pairs of opposites,
> stated in the right way, make a direct appeal to the
> normal habits of the mind.

Empson points out the following 'opposites' which
occur in lines 11-14 of the poem:

> *Weeping* produces the flowers of joy which are them-
> selves sorrowful; the *hill* is *green* as young, fresh and
> springing, or with age, mould and geology; *April* is
> both rainy and part of springtime; and the *shroud*, an
> anticipation of death that has its own energy and
> beauty, either is itself the fact that the old *hill* is
> hidden under *green*, or is itself the grey mist, the grey-
> ness of falling rain, which is reviving that verdure.

(*Seven Types of Ambiguity*, Chatto and Windus, 1930;
rev. edn., 1947, p. 215)

1-5. Yew is planted in churchyards and the seeds are
poisonous. The root of wolf's-bane (aconite) and the
berries of nightshade contain poisons which could take
one off to the Underworld ruled over by Pluto and
Proserpine, his wife. Lethe is a river in the Underworld.
6. The death-watch beetle and the death's-head moth,
both ominous, are referred to.
7. *Your mournful Psyche*: Melancholy is seen, throughout
the poem, as a being to whom devout observances are
made. She has a shrine in a temple (stanza 3) where

trophies are hung (just as coats of arms are sometimes **89** hung as memorials in churches or represented on memorial tablets). In the first stanza, the 'wine' of lines 1-2, the chaplet of lines 3-4, the 'rosary' of line 5, the 'mysteries' of line 8, are all associated with religious observance, though some of these devotional aids are Christian and others pagan. In the *Ode to Psyche*, the goddess is the recipient of Keats's devotions, and the 'mournful Psyche' of this stanza (death) is the recipient of devotions paid in the melancholy state. 'Psyche' in Greek means 'soul' and 'moth,' so the death's-head moth is the representative of the 'mournful Psyche' (see H. W. Garrod, *Keats*, p. 100).

16. The spectrum of colours sometimes seen in wet sea-sand.

17. *globed peonies*: F. R. Leavis says:

> ... the hand is round the peony, luxuriously cupping it. Such tactual effects are notoriously characteristic of Keats, and they express, not merely the voluptuary's itch to be fingering, but that strong grasp upon actualities—upon things outside himself, that firm sense of the solid world, which makes Keats so different from Shelley.

> (*Revaluation*, pp. 261-2)

21. *She*: Melancholy, who is personified as a goddess.   **90**
24. *bee-mouth*: The bee cannot help searching for nectar, just as we cannot help seeking what would gratify us, and like ourselves, the bee goes intently and unthinkingly about its search. The associations of 'mouth' and of the heavily sweet nectar which the bee sips are such that they maintain the luxurious sensuousness of the preceding stanza. Notice that Keats usually appeals to more than one sense at a time, so that his images have depth. For instance, gazing into the eyes of the 'mistress' in lines 18-20 is accompanied by the feel of her soft hand, the experience is described as a 'feeding,' and it is both prolonged and intensified by the words 'deep, deep.'
30. *cloudy trophies*: Gloomy memorials of those who have been overcome.

Keats started writing this unfinished epic in the latter part of September 1818, and probably completed the first two books by the beginning of December, continuing to work on the third book until April 1819. It is, then, one of the earliest poems to be written for this volume. In August and September 1819, after he had completed all the verse included in *Poems of 1820* except Part II of *Lamia* and *To Autumn*, Keats made a fresh start with *Hyperion*, entitling it *The Fall of Hyperion*. This later version, which was not published in his lifetime, is given in this volume (p. 117). In *Hyperion* Keats proposed to deal with the displacement of the Titans by the Olympian gods, and more particularly with the supplanting of Hyperion, god of the sun, by Apollo, his Olympian counterpart. The Titans are dim figures, whose story is passed down from pre-Hellenic times. They were the offspring of Heaven and Earth and in Keats's poem Coelus (Heaven) assists his son Hyperion. In myth, the Olympian gods are, most of them, the offspring of the leader of the Titans (Saturn) and his sister (Ops). Under the leadership of Jupiter these children drive the older generation from their thrones to establish the Olympian hierarchy, with Jupiter as the new King of Heaven. At the time described in the poem the Titans have been overthrown, all except the sun god, Hyperion, and like Milton's fallen angels they have been driven into a place of darkness where they rally themselves for a counter-attack. It is a visit from Hyperion that puts fresh spirit into the Titans, though he too feels that he is losing his power, and in the third book we are introduced to his successor, Apollo, who is being changed into a god by the Titaness Mnemosyne. These events are partly legendary, partly made up by Keats, and if he had finished his poem it would, presumably, have dealt with the final subjugation of the Titans and the establishment of Apollo as god of the sun, of music, prophecy and medicine.

Hyperion is Keats's third long poem. The first was

Endymion, mostly written during 1817, a long, rather **91** rambling work of four thousand lines, which Keats himself thought immature. The second long poem is *Isabella,* which appears in this volume. These two earlier poems are works of sentiment—neither could satisfy Keats's desire to write an epic in the grand manner of Homer, Virgil, Dante or Milton—and *Hyperion,* it was hoped, would give him a subject with enough scope. Eight months before starting the poem Keats wrote in a letter:

> . . . in Endymion I think you may have many bits of the deep and sentimental cast—the nature of *Hyperion* will lead me to treat it in a more naked and grecian Manner—and the march of passion and endeavour will be undeviating—and one great contrast between them will be—that the Hero of the written tale [*Endymion*] being mortal is led on, like Buonaparte, by circumstance; whereas the Apollo in Hyperion being a fore-seeing God will shape his actions like one.
>
> (*To B. R. Haydon,* 23 January 1818)

Perhaps Keats is too ambitious in the intention he states here. Even Milton's epic is basically about mankind, not about 'fore-seeing Gods,' but it is clear that Keats wishes to escape from the limitations imposed on him by the conventions of poetry of his own time. In another letter he draws a distinction between the verse of Milton and of Wordsworth: Milton was contented with his 'resting places and seeming sure points of Reasoning' (content with a philosophical or godlike view of things), whereas Wordsworth, who presents his own emotions, 'martyrs himself to the human heart, the main region of his song' (*To J. H. Reynolds,* 3 May 1818). Keats's dissatisfaction with Wordsworthian 'limitations' is more plainly stated in the letter to Reynolds (3 February 1818) partly quoted in the notes on *Lines on the Mermaid Tavern* (see pp. 175-6). He complains that Wordsworth and Hunt are continually holding out for our inspection their personal feelings and the subjective significance of their experiences instead of taking a larger view. 'Why

91 should we be owls,' he asks, 'when we can be Eagles?' At the time of writing the first *Hyperion* Keats was attracted by the idea of describing something grandly aloof, archetypal or, at the least, universal—of depicting the human heart rather than a particular heart—but his normal impulse was to describe his own fears and desires and vivid impressions. When he comes to revise *Hyperion* we find him returning to his usual manner of writing and considering the subject, originally planned to follow the actions of a 'fore-seeing God,' from a more personal point of view; in terms of his own aspirations and the impressions made on his own sensibilities.

Kenneth Muir, in his chapter 'The Meaning of "Hyperion",' says:

> Although Keats may not at the time have been fully conscious of the identification, there is no doubt that his account of the deification of Apollo by disinterested suffering is a symbolic presentation of the 'dreamer' becoming a great poet. But the reference is wider. Keats, in his famous parable, wrote of the world, not as a vale of tears, but as a vale of soul-making; so that the deification of Apollo is symbolic of the birth of a soul in all who are thus reborn . . . This description of 'dying into life' is the conclusion of the poem. When Keats had written so far he handed the manuscript to Woodhouse, realizing that he had reached the limit of his experience.
>
> (*John Keats: A Reassessment*, p. 108)

Hyperion, Muir says,

> is only superficially about the ancient gods: its real subject, as we have seen, is human progress; and the new race of men imagined by the poet were not stronger or cleverer than their predecessors, but more sensitive and vulnerable—not characters, but personalities. The weaknesses of the poem, apart from its too Miltonic style, are that Keats's narrative power is only intermittently displayed; the rhythmical impetus frequently exhausts itself at the end of a paragraph;

and the fable itself is not perfectly adapted to the **91** meaning Keats tried to impose on it. It was in an attempt to remedy these faults that he began to recast the poem in the summer of 1819.

(op. cit., p. 109)

In attempting to recast the poem, however, Keats:

realized that he could never finish *The Fall of Hyperion,* for a reason obvious enough but never mentioned by him: he had already used up the climax of the first poem in the first canto of the second version.

(op. cit., p. 120)

Book I

13. *Naiad*: The nymph, spirit of the stream.

21. *His ancient mother*: Saturn was born of the Heavens (Coelus) and the Earth (Tellus).

26. *the infant world*: According to the poets the overthrow of Saturn ended the Golden Age, when men lived peaceably without laws on the natural abundance of the earth.

27. *the tall Amazon*: The female warriors of Greek **92** legend.

30. *Ixion's wheel*: As punishment for his crimes when alive, Ixion was bound to a burning wheel which turned for ever.

31. *Memphian*: Memphis was the second city of ancient Egypt.

32-3. The sphinx was mounted on a pedestal at the time when Egypt was one of the chief centres of learning in the world. This sort of circumstantial detail built into the imagery, almost as a digression, is characteristic of Milton and the classical epics, and it is to be noticed that Keats adopts a digressive manner in this poem, together with other epic devices. Milton's excursions are often very lengthy.

39-41. The 'van' and 'rear' of an army are the advance forces and the hindmost portion. In this image, the rear

92 is seen as still to come, carrying with it heavier and more devastating weapons.

49-51. The 'utterance' of the goddess is greater than can be rendered in the 'frail' language of men. Milton encounters the same difficulty when Raphael exclaims to Adam:

> Sad task and hard, for how shall I relate
> To human sense th' invisible exploits
> Of warring Spirits . . .
>
> (*Paradise Lost*, V, 564)

56. *Knows thee not, thus afflicted*: The wording imitates Latin. Latin constructions are a mannerism in the poem indicative of the influence of Milton. In preparation for the writing of *Hyperion*, Keats studied both Dante (in Henry Cary's translation) and Milton.

60-3. *Thy thunder . . . And thy sharp lightning*: When sovereignty over the Heavens passed to Jupiter he assumed control of the weapons of Saturn.

93 64-7. When we are afflicted by grief time passes slowly. The goddess states that the slow passage of time augments the grief of the Titans.

72-9. The comparison has Miltonic weight and stateliness.

74. *branch-charmed*: The unmoving stars seem to have cast a spell on the trees, immobilizing them. These words, and other words in the image ('tranced' and 'dream') maintain the impression of Saturn's dazed state.

83-4. *One moon . . . had shed/Her silver seasons four*: A month passed by, with the four phases of the moon.

86. *cathedral cavern*: An enormous cave.

87. *couchant*: Lying down. The heraldic overtones of the word emphasize the statuesque postures of the Titans.

94 102. *front*: The forehead. The word is chosen, like many others in this section, to heighten the idea of monolithic grandeur.

105. *nervous*: Muscular. Saturn had supposed himself the master of Fate.

107-8. Jupiter has assumed control of the heavenly bodies.

109. *admonitions*: Commands.

94

117. *sphere*: The word is chosen to give magnitude to the action. The movements of the eye are related to the movements of the universe.

118. *lorn of light*: Beyond the light of the stars.

124-5. *it must/Be ripe of progress*: It must be well on the way to fulfilment.

127. *There must be Gods thrown down*: Saturn anticipates the overthrow of the Olympian gods who had displaced the Titans.

129. *metropolitan*: The metropolis or capital city of the gods is situated in the skies. The word order in this line is Latinate.

130. *proclaim*: The voices will be sounds proclaiming the victory Saturn expects.

131. *strings in hollow shells*: Primitive stringed instruments.

133. *sky-children*: The Titans, offspring of the Heavens.

95

137. *Druid locks*: The Druids were priests of Celtic times, usually depicted as old men with flowing hair and beards.

138. *fever out*: His eyes are prominent and glistening, as if he were fevered.

145. *Chaos*: Keats here depicts Saturn as the creator of the ordered universe. Ovid describes Chaos as the raw material of the universe: 'a shapeless, uncoordinated mass, nothing but a weight of lifeless matter, whose ill-assorted elements were indiscriminately heaped together in one place' (*Metamorphoses*, Book I). In the 1820 edition of the poems, 'Chaos' is spelt without a capital here and in Book II, line 191. The spelling has been altered to conform with spelling elsewhere in the poem. The alteration conforms, also, with Keats's autograph. 'Darkness' (II, 191) and 'Light' (II, 195) are capitalized for the same reason.

147. *The rebel three*: Jupiter (Jove), supreme ruler of Heaven; Neptune, god of the sea; Pluto, ruler of the Underworld. All three are sons of Saturn.

150. *house*: The Titan dynasty.

152. *covert*: The place where the Titans are sheltering.

NOTES

95 160. Cf. lines 50-1.

164. *But one*: Only one.

96 166. *orbed fire*: The sphere of the sun, as Hyperion is the sun god.

167. *incense*: Which is burned on the altars dedicated to him on earth.

171. *gloom-bird*: The owl, which is a bird of ill omen.

172-3. The visit of a ghost is referred to.

174. Occult warnings obtained by witchcraft.

175. *portion'd*: Proportioned.

176-82. The 'palace' of the sun is in the West (or East) and so it is described here in terms of a flaming sunset (or sunrise). Aurora is the dawn. An 'obelisk' is a tapering stone monument.

192. *For rest*: Instead of taking his rest.

197-200. The comparison is Miltonic, partly because it is digressive, partly because of the cleverly managed shift in perspective. The minions (dependents) are thrown abruptly into the distance, seen as small figures in a wide threatening landscape. This emphasizes their helplessness, it magnifies the stature of Hyperion, and it echoes the shaken world of the Titans. Keats greatly admired Milton's control of such 'staged' effects, and wrote in his copy of Milton: 'Milton . . . pursues his imagination to the utmost . . . in no instance is this sort of perseverance more exemplified than in what may be called his stationing or statuary.' In *Hyperion* Keats places his figures in impressive postures, often maintaining them there for a length of time, and also gives them imposing settings, usually conveying the mood of the figure indirectly by means of the setting.

97 204. *slope*: Sloping down. Cf. *The Fall of Hyperion*, II, 48.

205-8. The subdued stateliness of sunset provides the setting (see lines 197-200, note). A mechanism operated by the gates of the West causes the light evening winds ('Zephyrs') to blow musically across a pipe instrument ('tubes'), welcoming the god (cf. *Lamia*, I, 386-8). Milton might have written these lines, though only Keats would have made the comparison that follows (209-12).

216. *Hours*: Goddesses of the seasons attendant on the 97
sun.

226. *curb*: His restraint.

231. *Why do I know ye?*: Hyperion asks why it is that he
has come to have visions of horrible forms.

232. *essence*: Spiritual 'substance.'

238. *fanes*: Temples. 98

244. *shady visions*: See lines 227-30.

246. *Tellus*: Hyperion's mother, the Earth, who is
'clothed' in the sea.

249. *Jove*: The newly enthroned Jupiter who now con-
trols the weapons of Saturn, thunder and lightning.

255. *Phantoms*: Those mentioned in lines 227-31.

264-89. These lines are Miltonically splendid, leisurely
and digressive. As Keats depicts Hyperion, he rides on
the 'planet orb' of the sun through the 'eastern gates' of
the dawn each morning. The sun is equipped with two
silver wings, though not because it needs them (283-5),
and during the night it is hidden behind black clouds
(271). Even when the sun is hidden, however, some light
breaks from it which men see as polar lights and other
luminous phenomena which, by long observation (280),
wise men were once able to interpret like 'hieroglyphics.'
This astrological wisdom has been lost though archaeo-
logists find records of it (281-3). Lines of 'colure' (274)
pass through the poles.

288. *maintain'd eclipse*: Remained hidden from the 99
world.

291. *if but for change*: Even if only for the sake of a new
activity, which would bring him relief.

296. *sisterly*: In close relationship to each other.

298. *demesnes*: Territories.

299. *phrenzied*: Made frantic.

300. *Unus'd to bend*: Unused to bow his will.

302. *rack*: The clouds are broken by storm.

309-19. Coelus, the Heavens, and Tellus, the Earth, are 100
the 'powers' which engendered the Titans (the 'fruits'),
but Coelus is aware of a force superior to himself, a
'beauteous life/Diffus'd unseen throughout eternal
space' (317-18). Thus Hyperion is the 'Son of Mys-

100 teries' (310) which Coelus cannot fathom. Oceanus, whom we meet in Book III, is also aware of the purposes of a larger force.

322. *Of son against his sire*: Of Jupiter against Saturn, who tumbles from his throne.

326. *wox*: Became. Coelus is very old and uses a quaintly archaic-sounding word coined by Keats as the past tense of 'wax.'

330. *sad*: Serious or mature.

343-5. Hyperion must be beforehand with events, must prevent the flight of the arrow aimed at him.

101 **349.** *region-whisper*: Because Coelus is a place, his message is not delivered in speech.

Book II

The events of this book have many parallels in Books I and II of *Paradise Lost*.

4. *Cybele*: Ops, wife of Saturn.

5. *insulting light*: Cf. line 366, note, p. 192.

9. In the constant roar of waters it cannot be determined where they go.

14. *nest*: Used in its depreciatory sense, as in 'nest of thieves' or 'snakes.'

102 **19 ff.** Some of the Titans are correctly called by names that are traditional, some are incorrectly given the names of Giants, and some names are introduced by Keats.

22. *regions of laborious breath*: These are stifled in the entrails of the earth.

28. *gurge*: A swirling. The word is Miltonic.

29. *Mnemosyne*: See Book III, line 77, note.

33-8. See Book I, lines 197-200, note.

39. *kept shroud*: They cover their heads in their attire. This is a place of mourning.

45. *plashy*: Marked as if splashed with colour.

103 **56-63.** Asia is depicted as the future goddess of an eastern cult.

69-72. Perhaps it was Keats's intention to deal with this **103** 'second war' in a later book. In legend a later war was waged against Jupiter by the Giants, who piled mountains on top of each other in order to reach Olympus. Keats takes the Titans and the Giants as being identical. In *Paradise Lost* mountains are thrown during the war in Heaven.

82-3. The muse of poetry is eager to proceed with the story.

98. *disanointing poison*: Because he has been made mortal, **104** Saturn is deprived of godhood and of kingship.

116-28. See Book I, lines 197-200, note.

120. *utterless*: Because the thoughts are too deep for words, but also because the thoughts of a god cannot be conveyed in mere language.

129-55. This sentence has a truly Miltonic amplitude, as **105** befits the utterance of a god. Saturn first refers to his inability to account for the plight of the Titans by reading the incorporeal book (133) discovered by his father Uranus (i.e. Coelus) in the shallows of the sea of light (135-6). He goes on to talk of his inability to account for their state by reading the signs of Nature, which are 'written' in the changing conditions of the elements (earth, fire, air and water).

161. *engine*: Put into effective action.

168. *from no Athenian grove*: The wisdom of Oceanus **106** has not been gained by attendance at an academy of ancient Greece.

170. *not oozy*: Because he is out of his watery element.

171-2. His speech came, at first, in imitation of the sound of sea breakers.

176. *bellows*: To blow the fires of wrath.

183. *sifted*: Closely examined. Cf. lines 139-51.

186. *avenue*: Way to the truth.

190-7. The passage owes something to the opening of Book III of *Paradise Lost*, which is itself indebted to *Genesis* i and *John* i. The 'intestine broil' (192) and 'sullen ferment' (193) refer to the warring of the amorphous elements in Chaos.

191. *Chaos . . . Darkness*: See Book I, line 145, note.

107 205. *top of sovereignty*: The height of kingliness.

207. *chiefs*: Predominant in the universe.

208. *show beyond*: Are evidently superior to.

217-23. As Oceanus is making an inspired pronouncement, he speaks with the inflexions of the Book of Job.

108 232. *young God of the Seas*: Neptune.

244. *poz'd*: Certain.

248. *Clymene*: Even the legends are vague about her identity.

250. *hectic*: Fevered.

109 277. Her hearing was altogether given up to the sound by which it was so enlivened.

281. Compare Keats's response in the *Ode to a Nightingale*.

289. Cf. line 281.

293. *Apollo*: Hyperion's successor, whom we meet in Book III.

110 304. *Enceladus*: In myth, one of the Giants who later rose against Jupiter. See lines 69-72, note.

309-10. Oceanus and Clymene are referred to.

320. *Thy scalding*: The seas were heated by thunderbolts thrown by Jupiter.

328. *ether*: The element filling upper space where the gods lived.

329. *crooked stings*: Lightning flashes.

335-6. See the description of Enceladus in lines 64-72. When Saturn was deposed the Age of Gold was concluded, an age when bloodshed and injustice were unknown.

111 341. *winged thing*: The goddess of victory is often depicted with wings.

366. *made it terrible*: The light is terrible because of what it reveals.

370. Notice the Latin construction.

371. Numidia was on the north coast of Africa.

112 374-7. Memnon was a legendary king of Ethiopia or Egypt. The colossi of Memnon were said to make a mournful sound at dusk.

3-6. The atmosphere of this unfinished book is different from that of the first two. It is elevated, but not in the grandly orchestrated, aloof manner of Milton. Instead there is a return to the soul searchings and sensuous involvement of *Endymion*. Keats anticipates this in these lines. At the time that the Book was being written Keats was also producing *The Eve of St. Agnes* and the Odes, which are decidely not in the spirit of the first two Books of *Hyperion*, and when he came to write the revised *Hyperion* he no longer attempted the detached epic manner.

10-28. We now come to deal with the metamorphosis of Apollo into a god, and the setting is Delos (23-7), his birthplace, one of the Aegean islands called the Cyclades. As well as being the god of the sun, of music (13), medicine, and animal husbandry, Apollo is associated with prophecy, and his chief oracular shrine was at Delphi (10), a most important religious centre. Because Keats's theme now takes him to the times of classical Greece he invokes the Dorian flute (12), in place of the primitive instruments we have heard—strings in hollow shells (I, 131), and the shell of Clymene (II, 270). Keats associates Apollo with the colour red (14-22), and it is for this reason that he refers specifically to 'the clouds of even and of morn' (16), which are tinged with that colour.

31. *mother fair*: The Titaness Leto.   113
32. *twin-sister*: Artemis (or Diana), goddess of the moon and of the chase.

77. The speaker is the Titaness Mnemosyne (see II, 29)   114 who has deserted Saturn for love of Apollo. She is memory, mother of the muses.

87. *oblivion*: Ignorance.   115

92-3. *the liegeless air/Yields to my step aspirant*: The air knows no master and will not support his attempts to ascend.

130. *Die into life*: In dying, be transformed.   116

K.P.   193   G

Appendix

THE FALL OF HYPERION

Keats set aside the first version of *Hyperion* in April 1819 before writing the Odes. In late July (having completed the first part of *Lamia*) he took up the poem again and revised it to produce *The Fall of Hyperion*. This fresh attempt to complete the poem was also abandoned, and he made no serious attempt to complete it after 21 September when he wrote to John Hamilton Reynolds:

> I have given up Hyperion—there were too many Miltonic inversions in it—Miltonic verse can not be written but in an artful or rather artist's humour. I wish to give myself up to other sensations. English ought to be kept up.

The last sentence is best explained by quoting from a letter written on the same day to his brother George:

> The Paradise lost though so fine in itself is a curruption of our Language—it should be kept as it is unique—a curiosity—a beautiful and grand Curiosity. The most remarkable Production of the world. A northern dialect accommodating itself to greek and latin inversions and intonations. The purest english I think—or what ought to be the purest—is Chatterton's. The Language had existed long enough to be entirely uncorrupted of Chaucer's gallicisms, and still the old words are used. Chatterton's language is entirely northern. I prefer the native music of it to Milton's cut by feet. I have but lately stood on my guard against Milton. Life to him would be death to me.

The difficulty with Milton's style cannot be regarded as the only problem Keats was confronted with in attempting to complete the poem, however. The subject he chose is a difficult one—there is no successful piece of writing that concerns itself exclusively with the interests of supernatural beings—not even Milton attempted such a subject, and once Keats had completed the really new part of the revised *Hyperion* he found himself with his old subject on his hands again with its fundamentally unmanageable material. What is interesting about the later addition is that it does deal directly with the human, with Keats himself and with his primary interest: the nature of poetry and of the poet. Indeed, some critics consider the addition to be the most valuable thing Keats ever wrote. J. Middleton Murry, for instance, says that it is 'the profoundest and most sublime of his poems' (*Keats and Shakespeare*, p. 169).

Despite the excellence of *The Fall of Hyperion* it was not published during Keats's lifetime. The original *Fragment* was included in the *Poems of 1820*, his last volume, but the revised version lay among his literary remains until it was published by Monckton Milnes in 1856. Even Keats's own manuscript of *The Fall of Hyperion* is lost, and the present version is based on a copy of the poem made by Richard Woodhouse, a friend and admirer of Keats who carefully transcribed much of his verse.

At the beginning of *The Fall of Hyperion* Keats finds himself in a pleasant garden surrounded by every kind of abundance, and from there he is transported to an enormous gloomy temple. Some help in interpreting this allegorical description of the progress of the soul may be obtained from a letter Keats wrote a year before to Reynolds. The pleasant garden at the beginning of the poem is roughly equivalent to the 'Chamber of Maiden-Thought' described in the letter, though Keats's ideas have developed in the intervening year. He wrote:

I compare human life to a large Mansion of Many Apartments, two of which I can only describe, the doors of the rest being as yet shut upon me. The first we step into we call the infant or thoughtless Chamber, in which we remain as long as we do not think . . . we no sooner get into the second Chamber, which

117   I shall call the Chamber of Maiden-Thought, than we become intoxicated with the light and the atmosphere, we see nothing but pleasant wonders, and think of delaying there for ever in delight: However among the effects this breathing is father of is that tremendous one of sharpening one's vision into the heart and nature of Man—of convincing one's nerves that the world is full of Misery and Heartbreak, Pain, Sickness and oppression—whereby this Chamber of Maiden Thought becomes gradually darken'd and at the same time on all sides of it many doors are set open—but all dark—all leading to dark passages. We see not the balance of good and evil. We are in a Mist. *We* are now in that state—We feel the 'burden of the Mystery' . . .

(3 May 1818)

The first *Hyperion* was influenced by Dante, though to a lesser degree than by Milton. The only book taken by Keats on his Scottish walking tour, undertaken just before writing the poem, was a miniature three-volume edition of Henry Cary's translation of Dante, written in Miltonic blank verse. The influence of Dante on the second *Hyperion* is more marked. M. R. Ridley says,

it is difficult to resist the impression that *The Fall of Hyperion* owed more to Dante than a few phrases. The whole conception of the dream is that of Dante, though no doubt plenty of poets have written visions.

(*Keats' Craftsmanship*, p. 271)

F. R. Leavis contrasts the verse of the revised version with that of the first:

it lacks entirely the epic (if rather languid) buoyancy, the Miltonic wave-motion, the onward-carrying rise and fall [of the first *Hyperion*] . . . The new verse moves line by line, the characteristic single line having, as it were, an evenly distributed weight—a settled, quite unspringy balance. It is this peculiar rhythmic character that had led one to divine, as an influence in this technical development, a study of Dante in the 117 Italian (Cary could hardly have had much to do with so extraordinary a change as that represented by the new verse compared with the earlier).

(*Revaluation*, p. 269)

Leavis continues:

Dante, of course, for Keats was not a technical study, and was something more than literature. What the strength of the influence, the intensity of the effect, shows is how much the study was part of the discipline and self-searching with which Keats met the disasters, the blows of fate, that were making life for him overwhelmingly a matter of 'the agonies, the strife of human hearts.' The immediately personal urgency of the preoccupation with suffering and death comes out plainly in the passage describing his nightmare race against the burning of the 'gummed leaves' (106-34). But this personal urgency is completely impersonalized; it has become the life, the informing spirit, of the profoundest kind of impersonality.

(*op. cit.*, p. 270)

The original version of the poem is referred to as *Hyperion* in the notes that follow.

Canto I

1-18. Poetry and religious vision have always been associated with each other. The early poets were prophets and the drama has its origins in religious festival. Keats bases the passage on this fact, referring to the fanatic who sounds like poet and prophet though his message is spurious, and the savage whose religion is not quite poetry (6) because not fully articulate (is 'dumb enchantment') as well as being unrecorded (4 and 5). The 'sable charm' (10) probably refers to the necromantic practices of primitive superstitions. Keats concludes by asserting the right of every man to tell his visions. Posterity will determine whether the vision is

117 true or false, is inspired poetry or delusion. In this edition a full stop has been added at the end of line 15.

118 27. The flowers, swung on their stems, give out fragrance, just as a censer, swung on its chain, gives out clouds of incense.

35-8. The horn is the Cornucopia, from which the fruits of the earth flow. It is associated with Ceres, the corn-goddess, whose daughter Proserpine was taken off to Hades by Pluto. When Proserpine returns to the earth, as she is permitted to do for six months of the year, Ceres allows the earth to be fruitful. The classical allusion is used here in a much more extended manner than in (say) *Lamia*, II, 187.

46. *is parent of my theme*: Gives rise to what follows.

47-50. The Caliphs were the rulers of the Mohammedan world after the death of the Prophet. The 'scarlet conclave' is the assemblage of Cardinals. By repute, the court of the Caliphs and the palaces of the Cardinals in Renaissance times were centres of intrigue where the administration of poison to rivals was much resorted to. The Caliphs were 'soon fading' because short-lived.

56. *Silenus*: See *Lamia*, I, 103, note. The Sileni, as followers of Bacchus, are often depicted in a drunken torpor.

119 70. *faulture*: Decayed remnants.

79-80. These were appurtenances of religious rites in classical times.

92. *degrees*: Steps.

120 97-105. The extended Miltonic simile used here is not characteristic of the additions made to the poem and Keats omitted some that he had made earlier. Compare, for instance, lines 336-8 in this canto with *Hyperion*, I, 26-36.

103. *Maian*: Maia is the goddess of May.

116. *gummed leaves*: The leaves of some tree containing an odorous gum.

121 135. The angels of Jacob's dream are referred to.

137. *horned shrine*: The altar with its projections. Cf. line 237.

144. *dated on*: Postponed.

148-9. Cf. Keats's letter quoted in the introduction to 121
the notes on this poem, pp. 195-6.

152. *fane*: Temple.

161-2. Cf. lines 1-18.

169. *A fever of thyself*: In fever, hallucinations are ex- 122
perienced.

179. See lines 19-39.

183-5. She has been diagnosing his illness—an illness of
which he need not be ashamed. Indeed he feels that her
words do him honour.

187-210. These lines do not appear in the version of the
poem printed by Monckton Milnes in 1857, and in the
Woodhouse transcript there is a note saying that Keats
'seems to have intended to erase' the lines. The argu-
ments as to whether Keats intended to delete the lines
or not are given in J. M. Murry's *Keats*, Chapter IX.
Lines 194-8, it will be noticed, are repeated later as lines
216-20, and so are the words 'Majestic shadow' in lines
187 and 211. These repetitions make it probable that
Keats deleted the lines and used part of them in re-
writing. E. de Sélincourt argues that the lines are
necessary to complete the argument about the difference
between poet and dreamer (*The Poems of John Keats*,
'The Fall of Hyperion—Notes'). J. M. Murry argues
that Keats was free of the false modesty implied in the
lines.

202-6. Keats shouts with the frenzied anger of the
priestess ('Pythia') who acted as oracle of Apollo at
Delphi. He calls on Apollo (see *Hyperion*, III, 10-28,
note) because he is the god of plagues as well as of
poetry, and can be expected to punish with 'pestilence'
those who desecrate his art.

208. *Hectorers*: Blusterers. Keats may have had Byron in 123
mind.

226. *Saturn*: The leader of the Titans. See introductory
note to *Hyperion*.

226. *Moneta*: She is later addressed as Mnemosyne (331),
and it is under that name that she appears in *Hyperion*
(see III, 77, note). Moneta is a Roman goddess of
admonition.

NOTES

123 233. *sweet food*: Sweetly scented fuel.

124 245. *swooning*: The scenes are not faint. They are so vivid that they cause the mind to feel faint.

246. *electral*: Charged.

249. *sphered*: Set among the spheres—heavenly.

261-2. *it had pass'd/The lily and the snow*: Her face was white ('blanch'd') beyond the whiteness of the lily and snow.

272. The 'grain of gold' is an indication of seams of gold within the mountain.

125 281. *planetary eyes*: Cf. lines 268-71.

282. *'Shade of Memory!'*: She is to impart the incidents she remembers, but this is also a way of addressing her by her name: Mnemosyne, which means 'memory.'

286. See *Hyperion*, Book III.

288. *Omega*: The last representative. Omega is the last letter of the Greek alphabet.

294. At this line Keats introduces the material he first wrote for *Hyperion*. Some of it is identical, some has been altered, and there are interpolations every now and then.

308. *half unravel'd web*: The theme is likened to a woven fabric which must be unravelled if one wishes to understand how it is made.

126 317. *Naiad*: See *Hyperion*, I, 13, note.

326. *His antient mother*: See *Hyperion*, I, 21, note. Keats uses an old form of 'ancient.'

331. *Mnemosyne*: Keats's guide, previously addressed as Moneta. See *Hyperion*, III, 77, note.

336. *statuary*: Her stature is greater, but it is implied, also, that she is statuesque.

341-3. See *Hyperion*, I, 39-41, note.

127 351-3. See *Hyperion*, I, 49-51, note.

362-5. See *Hyperion*, I, 60-3, note. Keats has effected an improvement in substituting 'captious' for 'conscious.'

366-7. Cf. *Hyperion*, I, 64-7. The new version is less bombastic.

373. *branch-charmed*: See *Hyperion*, I, 74, note.

128 392. *moon*: A lunar month.

411. *Pan*: The goat-like god who inhabited rural places.

414. See *Hyperion*, I, 107-8, note. 128
423-4. The fall of Saturn marked the end of the Golden 129
Age, a time that was free of death and injustice.
425-6. Cybele is his wife, and their 'pernicious babes' are
Jupiter and the Olympian Gods who have overthrown
their father.
435. *proclaim*: See *Hyperion*, I, 130, note.
436. *strings in hollow shells*: See *Hyperion*, I, 131, note.
438. *the sky-children*: See *Hyperion*, I, 133, note.
441-5. The fine appearance of Saturn is at variance
with his pathetic tones.
462. *wait*: It is possible that Keats wrote 'waste,' though 130
'wait' seems more likely.

Canto II

13. *But*: See *Hyperion*, I, 164, note.
15. *orbed*: See *Hyperion*, I, 166, note.
16. *incense*: See *Hyperion*, I, 167, note. 131
18. *prodigies*: Unnatural events.
20. *gloom-bird*: See *Hyperion*, I, 171, note.
21-2. See *Hyperion*, I, 172-3, note.
23. *portion'd*: See *Hyperion*, I, 175, note.
24-30. See *Hyperion*, I, 176-82, note.
40-4. See *Hyperion*, I, 197-200, note.
60. *hours*: See *Hyperion*, I, 216, note. 132

Critical Extracts

Works listed in the Bibliography are given shortened titles here.

From Keats's Letters

JOHN KEATS

. . . several things dovetailed in my mind, and at once it struck me what quality went to form a Man of Achievement especially in Literature and which Shakespeare possessed so enormously—I mean *Negative Capability*, that is when man is capable of being in uncertainties, Mysteries, doubts, without any irritable reaching after fact and reason—Coleridge, for instance, would let go by a fine isolated verisimilitude caught from the Penetralium of mystery, from being incapable of remaining Content with half knowledge. This pursued through Volumes would perhaps take us no further than this, that with a great poet the sense of Beauty overcomes every other consideration, or rather obliterates all consideration.

Letter to George and Thomas Keats, 21 December 1817 (p.71)*

Memory should not be called knowledge. Many have original minds who do not think it—they are led away by Custom. Now it appears to me that almost any Man may like the spider spin from his own inwards his own airy Citadel—the points of leaves and twigs on which the spider begins her work are few, and she fills the air with a beautiful circuiting. Man should be content with as few points to tip with the fine Web of his Soul, and weave a tapestry empyrean full of symbols for his spiritual eye, of softness for his spiritual touch, of space for his wandering, of distinctness for his luxury.

Letter to J. H. Reynolds, 19 February 1818 (p.102)

*Page references in the quotations from Keats's letters are to *The Letters of John Keats*, ed. M. Buxton Forman (Oxford University Press, 1960 edn.).

In Poetry I have a few Axioms, and you will see how far I am from their Centre. 1st. I think Poetry should surprise by a fine excess and not by Singularity—it should strike the Reader as a wording of his own highest thoughts, and appear almost a Remembrance—2nd. Its touches of Beauty should never be half way thereby making the reader breathless instead of content: the rise, the progress, the setting of imagery should like the Sun come natural to him—shine over him and set soberly although in magnificence leaving him in the Luxury of twilight—but it is easier to think what Poetry should be than to write it—and this leads me on to another axiom. That if Poetry comes not as naturally as the Leaves to a tree it had better not come at all.

Letter to John Taylor, 27 February 1818 (p.107)

An extensive knowledge is needful to thinking people—it takes away the heat and fever; and helps, by widening speculation, to ease the Burden of the Mystery: a thing I begin to understand a little, and which weighed upon you in the most gloomy and true sentence in your Letter. The difference of high Sensations with and without knowledge appears to me this—in the latter case we are falling continually ten thousand fathoms deep and being blown up again without wings and with all the horror of a bare shouldered creature—in the former case, our shoulders are fledge, and we go thro' the same air and space without fear.

Letter to J. H. Reynolds, 3 May 1818 (p.139)

The common cognomen of this world among the misguided and superstitious is 'a vale of tears' from which we are to be redeemed by a certain arbitary interposition of God and taken to Heaven—What a little circumscribed straightened notion! Call the world if you Please 'The vale of Soul-making.' Then you will find out the use of the world (I am speaking now in the highest terms for human nature admitting it to be immortal which I will here take for granted for the purpose of showing a thought which has struck me concerning it) I say '*Soul making*' Soul as distinguished from an Intelligence—There may be intelligences or sparks of the divinity in millions—but they are not Souls till they acquire identities, till each one is personally itself . . . I will call the *world* a School instituted for the purpose of teaching little children to read—I will call the *human heart* the *horn Book* used in that School—and I will call the *Child able to read, the Soul* made from that *School* and its *hornbook.* Do you not see how necessary a World of Pains and troubles is to school an Intelligence and make it a Soul? A Place where the heart must feel and suffer in a thousand diverse ways. Not merely is the Heart a Hornbook, It is the Minds Bible, it is the Minds experience, it is the teat from which the Mind or intelligence sucks its identity. As various as the Lives of Men are—so various become their Souls, and thus does God make individual beings, Souls, Identical Souls of the Sparks of his own essence.

Letter to George and Georgiana Keats, 29 April 1819 (pp.334–5)

I received a copy of the Cenci, as from yourself from Hunt. There is only one part of it I am judge of; the Poetry, and dramatic effect, which by many spirits now a days is considered the mammon. A modern work it is said must have a purpose, which may be the God—*an artist* must serve Mammon—he must have 'self concentration' selfishness perhaps. You I am sure will forgive me for sincerely remarking that you might curb your magnanimity and be more of an artist, and 'load every rift' of your subject with ore. The thought of such discipline must fall like cold chains upon you, who perhaps never sat with your wings furl'd for six Months together. And is not this extraordinary talk for the writer of Endymion! whose mind was like a pack of scattered cards—I am pick'd up and sorted to a pip.

Letter to Percy Bysshe Shelley, 16 August 1820 (pp.507–8)

JOHN WILSON CROKER

It is not that Mr. Keats, (if that be his real name, for we almost doubt that any man in his senses would put his real name to such a rhapsody,) it is not, we say, that the author has not powers of language, rays of fancy, and gleams of genius

—he has all these; but he is unhappily a disciple of the new school of what has been somewhere called Cockney poetry; which may be defined to consist of the most incongruous ideas in the most uncouth language. . . . This author is a copyist of Mr. Hunt; but he is more unintelligible, almost as rugged, twice as diffuse, and ten times more tiresome and absurd than his prototype, who, though he impudently presumed to seat himself in the chair of criticism, and to measure his own poetry by his own standard, yet generally had a meaning. But Mr. Keats has advanced no dogmas which he was bound to support by examples; his nonsense therefore is quite gratuitous; he writes it for its own sake, and being bitten by Mr. Leigh Hunt's insane criticism, more than rivals the insanity of his poetry.

From a review of *Endymion* in *The Quarterly Review*, Vol. XIX, No. XXXVII, April 1818 (p.207)

JOHN GIBSON LOCKHART*

To witness the disease of any human understanding, however feeble, is distressing; but the spectacle of an able mind reduced to a state of insanity is of course ten times more afflicting. It is with such sorrow as this that we have contemplated the case of Mr. John Keats. . . . For some time we were in hopes, that he might get off with a violent fit or two; but of late the symptoms are terrible. The phrenzy of the 'Poems' was bad enough in its way; but it did not alarm us half so seriously as the calm, settled, imperturbable drivelling idiocy of 'Endymion.'

From 'The Cockney School of Poetry: No. IV' in *Blackwood's Edinburgh Magazine*, Vol. III, No. XVII, August 1818 (p.519)

JOHN KEATS

Praise or blame has but a momentary effect on the man whose love of beauty in the abstract makes him a severe critic on his own Works. My own domestic criticism has given me pain

*There is some doubt about the authorship of this passage as the article was not signed.

without comparison beyond what Blackwood or the Quarterly could possibly inflict, and also when I feel I am right, no external praise can give me such a glow as my own solitary reperception & ratification of what is fine. J.S. is perfectly right in regard to the slip-shod Endymion. That it is so is no fault of mine.—No!—though it may sound a little paradoxical. It is as good as I had power to make it—by myself. Had I been nervous about its being a perfect piece, & with that view asked advice, & trembled over every page, it would not have been written; for it is not in my nature to fumble—I will write independently.—I have written independently *without Judgment*.—I may write independently, & *with Judgment* hereafter. The Genius of Poetry must work out its own salvation in a man: It cannot be matured by law and precept, but by sensation & watchfulness in itself. That which is creative must create itself—In Endymion, I leaped headlong into the Sea, and thereby have become better acquainted with the Soundings, the quicksands, & the rocks, than if I had stayed upon the green shore, and piped a silly pipe, and took tea & comfortable advice.—I was never afraid of failure; for I would sooner fail than not be among the greatest.

Letter to J. A. Hessey, 9 October 1818 (p.221)

LEIGH HUNT

Endymion, with all its extraordinary powers, partook of the faults of youth, though the best ones; but the reader of Hyperion and these other stories [*Lamia*, etc.] would never guess that they were written at twenty. The author's versification is now perfected, the exuberances of his imagination restrained, and a calm power, the surest and loftiest of all power, takes place of the impatient workings of the younger god within him. The character of his genius is that of energy and voluptuousness, each able at will to take leave of the other, and possessing, in their union, a high feeling of humanity not common to the best authors who can less combine them.

Indicator, No. XLIV, 9 August 1820 (p.352)

FRANCIS JEFFREY

Mr. Keats, we understand, is still a very young man; and his whole works, indeed, bear evidence enough of the fact. They are full of extravagance and irregularity, rash attempts at originality, interminable wanderings, and excessive obscurity. They manifestly require, therefore, all the indulgence that can be claimed for a first attempt. But we think it no less plain that they deserve it: for they are flushed all over with the rich lights of fancy; and so coloured and bestrewn with the flowers of poetry, that even while perplexed and bewildered in their labyrinths, it is impossible to resist the intoxication of their sweetness, or to shut our hearts to the enchantments they so lavishly present.

. . . it must, we fear, be admitted, that, besides the riot and extravagance of his fancy, the scope and substance of Mr. Keats's poetry is rather too dreamy and abstracted to excite the strongest interest, or to sustain the attention through a work of any great compass or extent. He deals too much with shadowy and incomprehensible beings, and is too constantly rapt into an extra-mundane Elysium, to command a lasting interest with ordinary mortals—and must employ the agency of more varied and coarser emotions, if he wishes to take rank with the enduring poets of this or of former generations.

. . . There is a fragment of a projected Epic, entitled *Hyperion*, on the expulsion of Saturn and the Titanian deities by Jupiter and his younger adherents, of which we cannot advise the completion: for, though there are passages of some force and grandeur, it is sufficiently obvious, from the specimen before us, that the subject is too far removed from all the sources of human interest, to be successfully treated by any modern author. Mr. Keats has unquestionably a very beautiful imagination, a perfect ear for harmony, and a great familiarity with the finest diction of English poetry; but he must learn not to misuse or misapply these advantages; and neither to waste the good gifts of Nature and study on intractable themes, nor to luxuriate too recklessly on such as are more suitable.

From a review of *Endymion* and *Poems of 1820* in *The Edinburgh Review*, Vol. XXXIV, No. LXVII, August 1820 (p.203)

LORD BYRON

Pray send me *no more* poetry but what is rare and decidedly good. There is such a trash of Keats and the like upon my tables that I am ashamed to look at them. . . . No more Keats, I entreat;—flay him alive; if some of you don't I must skin him myself; there is no bearing the drivelling idiotism of the Mankin.

Letter to John Murray, 12 September 1820,
on receiving a copy of *Poems of 1820*

PERCY BYSSHE SHELLEY

Among modern things which have reached me is a volume of poems by Keats; in other respects insignificant enough, but containing the fragment of a poem called *Hyperion*. I dare say you have not time to read it; but it certainly is an astonishing piece of writing, and gives me a conception of Keats which I confess I had not before.

Letter to T. L. Peacock, 8 November 1820,
on receiving a copy of *Poems of 1820*

Posthumous Criticism

THOMAS DE QUINCEY

But Keats was an Englishman; Keats had the honour to speak the language of Chaucer, Shakespeare, Bacon, Milton, Newton. The more awful was the obligation of his allegiance. And yet upon his mother tongue, upon this English language, has Keats trampled as with the hoofs of a buffalo. With its syntax, with its prosody, with its idiom, he has played such fantastic tricks as could only enter into the heart of a barbarian, and for which only the anarchy of chaos could furnish a forgiving audience. Verily it required the *Hyperion* to weigh against the deep treason of these unparalleled offences.

'Notes on Gilfillan's "Gallery . . .,"'
Tait's Edinburgh Magazine, XIII, 1846 (p.249)
Reprinted in De Quincey's *Essays on the Poets*, Boston, 1853

RICHARD MONCKTON MILNES

I perceived that many, who heartily admired his poetry, looked on it as the production of a wayward, erratic genius, self-indulgent in conceits, disrespectful of the rules and limitations of Art, not only unlearned but careless of knowledge, not only exaggerated but despising proportion. I knew that his moral disposition was assumed to be weak, gluttonous of sensual excitement, querulous of severe judgment, fantastical in its tastes, and lackadaisical in its sentiments. He was all but universally believed to have been killed by a stupid savage article in a review . . . I had to show that Keats in his intellectual character, reverenced simplicity and truth above all things, and abhorred what was merely strange and strong —that he was ever learning and ever growing more conscious of his own ignorance—that his models were always the highest and the purest, and that his earnestness at aiming at their excellence was only equal to the humble estimation of his own efforts—that his poetical course was one of distinct and positive progress, exhibiting a self-command and self-direction which enabled him to understand and avoid the faults even of the writers he was most naturally inclined to esteem. . . . I had also to exhibit the moral peculiarities of Keats as the effects of a strong will, passionate temperament, indomitable courage, and a somewhat contemptuous disregard of other men—to represent him as unflinchingly meeting all criticism of his writings, and caring for the article, which was supposed to have had such homicidal success, just so far as it was an evidence of the little power he had as yet acquired over the sympathies of mankind, and no more. I had to make prominent the brave front he opposed to poverty and pain—to show how love of pleasure was in him continually subordinate to higher aspirations notwithstanding the sharp zest of enjoyment which his mercurial nature conferred on him; and above all, I had to illustrate how little he abused his full possession of that imaginative faculty, which enables the poet to vivify the phantoms of the hour, and to purify the objects of sense, beyond what the moralist may sanction, or the mere practical man can understand.

From the Preface to Life of Keats, 1848

Keats's Reputation in the Victorian Era

J. R. MACGILLIVRAY

The patronage of Keats by the Pre-Raphaelites did not prove to be entirely to the advantage of his reputation. No doubt their choice of subjects from his poems in the late forties and early fifties stimulated his growing vogue in artistic and *avant-garde* circles. [Holman] Hunt's picture from *The Eve of St. Agnes* which was exhibited at the Academy in 1848 attracted a good deal of attention in an important year for Keats's fame. Then when Rossetti and Morris began to publish poetry of their own it was increasingly apparent that the work of Keats was a great influence upon them. This, in a way, added to his prestige. But there was always the possibility that no distinction would be made between the earlier poet and his disciples, and that he would be more condemned for their extravagances than credited for their admired qualities. There was a real danger that he would be set down by their detractors as the founder of the 'Fleshly School of Poetry,' and that the pseudo-moral reprobation which Lockhart and Wilson had pronounced against Keats, as well as against [Leigh] Hunt, would be revived and given new credence. It was perhaps fortunate that, before Buchanan's assault on Rossetti, sentimental and feminine readers of poetry had discovered and adopted Keats. They did his reputation the greatest harm for a long time, but early in the eighteen-seventies they must have helped to protect it from direct attack. To revive Wilson's charge of 'pruriency' was to question the instinctive sympathies and the purity of taste of the Victorian lady.

Keats (p.lxi)

MATTHEW ARNOLD

This sensuous strain Keats had, and a man of his poetic powers could not, whatever his strain, but show his talent in it. But he has something more, and something better. We who believe Keats to have been by his promise, at any rate, if not fully by his performance, one of the very greatest of

English poets, and who believe also that a merely sensuous man cannot either by promise or by performance be a very great poet, because poetry interprets life, and so large and noble a part of life is outside of such a man's ken,—we cannot but look for signs in him of something more than sensuousness, for signs of character and virtue. And indeed the elements of high character Keats undoubtedly has, and the effort to develop them; . . . The truth is that 'the yearning passion for the Beautiful,' which was with Keats, as he himself truly says, the master-passion, is not a passion of the sensuous or sentimental man, is not a passion of the sensuous or sentimental poet. It is an intellectual and spiritual passion. It is 'connected and made one,' as Keats declares that in his case it was, 'with the ambition of the intellect.' It is, as he again says, 'the mighty *abstract idea* of Beauty in all things.' And in his last days Keats wrote: 'If I should die, I have left no immortal work behind me—nothing to make my friends proud of my memory; *but I have loved the principle of beauty in all things*, and if I had had time I would have made myself remembered.' He *has* made himself remembered, and remembered as no merely sensuous poet could be; and he has done it by having 'loved the principle of beauty in all things.'

For to see things in their beauty is to see things in their truth, and Keats knew it. 'What the Imagination seizes as Beauty must be Truth,' he says in prose; and in immortal verse he has said the same thing—

> 'Beauty is truth, truth beauty,—that is all
> Ye know on earth, and all ye need to know.'

No, it is not all; but it is true, deeply true, and we have deep need to know it. And with beauty goes not only truth, joy goes with her also; and this too Keats saw and said, as in the famous first line of his *Endymion* it stands written—

> 'A thing of beauty is a joy for ever.'

It is no small thing to have so loved the principle of beauty as to perceive the necessary relation of beauty with truth, and of both with joy. Keats was a great spirit, and counts for far more than many even of his admirers suppose, because this just and high perception made itself clear to him. Therefore a dignity and a glory shed gleams over his life, and happiness, too, was not a stranger to it. . . .

No one else in English poetry, save Shakespeare, has in expression quite the fascinating felicity of Keats, his perfection of loveliness. 'I think,' he said humbly, 'I shall be among the English poets after my death.' He is; he is with Shakespeare.

For the second great half of poetic interpretation, for that faculty of moral interpretation which is in Shakespeare, and is informed by him with the same power of beauty as his naturalistic interpretation, Keats was not ripe. For the architectonics of poetry, the faculty which presides at the evolution of works like the *Agamemnon* or *Lear*, he was not ripe. His *Endymion*, as he himself well saw, is a failure, and his *Hyperion*, fine things as it contains, is not a success. But in shorter things, where the matured power of moral interpretation, and the high architectonics which go with complete poetic development, are not required, he is perfect.

'John Keats', Ward's *English Poets*, 1880, Vol. IV (pp.427 ff.).
Essays in Criticism, Second Series, 1888 (pp.100 ff.)

SIR SIDNEY COLVIN

The influence, and something of the majesty, of *Paradise Lost* are in truth to be found in *Hyperion*: and the debate of the fallen Titans in the second book is obviously to some extent modelled on the debate of the fallen angels. But Miltonic the poem hardly is in any stricter sense. . . . in the matter of rhythm, Keats's blank verse has not the flight of Milton's. . . . As to diction and the poetic use of words, Keats shows almost as masterly an instinct as Milton himself: but while of Milton's diction the characteristic colour is derived from reading and meditation, from an impassioned conversance with the contents of books, the characteristic colour of Keats's diction is rather derived from conversance with nature and with the extreme refinements of physical sensation.
. . . He never writes for the eye merely, but vivifies everything he touches, telling even of dead and senseless things in terms of life, movement, and feeling. Thus the monuments in the chapel aisle [in *The Eve of St. Agnes*] are brought before us, not by any effort of description, but solely through our sym-

pathy with the shivering fancy of the beadsman. . . . When Madeline unclasps her jewels, a weaker poet would have dwelt on their lustre or other visible qualities: Keats puts those aside, and speaks straight to our spirits in an epithet breathing with the very life of the wearer,—'her warmed jewels.' . . . [The Odes] are written in a strain intense indeed, but meditative and brooding, and quite free from the declamatory and rhetorical elements which we are accustomed to associate with the idea of an ode.

Keats, 1887 (pp.158–70 *passim*)

ROBERT BRIDGES

[Keats has] the power of concentrating all the far-reaching resources of language on one point, so that a single and apparently effortless expression rejoices the aesthetic imagination at the moment when it is most expectant and exacting, and at the same time astonishes the intellect with a new aspect of truth. This is only found in the greatest poets, and is rare in them; and it is no doubt for the possession of this power that Keats has been often likened to Shakespeare.

John Keats, 1895. Reprinted as 'Introduction' to *The Poems of John Keats*, ed. G. Thorn Drury, 1896, Vol. I (p.xci)

Twentieth-Century Criticism

JOHN MIDDLETON MURRY

To use the terms which have been adopted from Keats himself, Keats abandoned the revised *Hyperion* because he was committing the sin of uttering soul-knowledge through an effort of mind-knowledge. . . . In other words, though the revised *Hyperion* is the profoundest of Keats's poems, it is not the most perfect, for it is but a partial and in a sense a forced expression of himself. We can learn from it his deepest and truest thoughts, but we shall not learn them as he would have had us learn them. His was a still deeper knowledge than that which he expressed in his abandoned poem: his knowledge was so deep and true that it did not need to be torn out of himself as this was. But to express his own knowledge completely in his own way was forbidden him by destiny: let us be thankful that the revised *Hyperion* remains. It was written in a fever. 'I want to compose without this fever,' he said to his brother after abandoning it, 'I hope one day I shall.' Nothing is more certain than that he would have done. The *Ode to Autumn* proves it.

Keats and Shakespear, 1925 (pp.69–70)

H. W. GARROD

... a passage [in *Sleep and Poetry*, published 1817] which has been much commented upon announces in very explicit terms the author's ambitions in poetry. He would wish 'for ten years' in which he may 'overwhelm' himself in an order of poetry of which the living figures are Flora and Pan and 'white-handed nymphs in shady places,' with one or another of whom the poet will play at kisses or at books, or dance or tame a dove, or wander on and on

> Through almond blossoms and rich cinnamon,
> Till in the bosom of a leafy world
> We rest in silence, like two gems upcurled
> In the recesses of a pearly shell.

That poetry, *that* Keats, we know well, and the affinity of his genius with this luxury of sensuous impressions. But he has wider and deeper ambitions in poetry; and in what follows, he makes confident revelation of them:

> And can I ever bid these joys farewell?
> Yes, I must pass them for a nobler life,
> Where I may find *the agonies, the strife*
> *Of human hearts.*

Thus early does he feel himself summoned out of his proper world. Something more upon this subject I shall say later. But it is proper, here and now, to mark in him this fitful setting of his temperament towards a world where I conceive him to have, in fact, very little business, a world which touches our world, the crying and striving of our politics, our social misery.

Not in political thinking, nor in tears given to human suffering, but in something which, though it seems easier, is, in fact, far harder, lies Keats' real effectiveness; in the exercise, I mean, of the five senses. As I say, it *seems* easier. Yet how few take trouble with it, how few manage it efficiently; how few, in comparison with the many who, in the enthusiasm of humanity, or in practical social zeal, are at least creditable practitioners!

Keats, 1926 (pp.29–30)

M. R. RIDLEY

For all that Keats is in some ways the most 'personal' of poets, yet in all his great work nothing is more remarkable than the way in which he stands aside, and allows, for example, the Nightingale to work her own way with us; we forget to admire the artistry in the beauty. There is the embalmed darkness, there is the song of the nightingale, and there are we; but Keats has withdrawn to watch his magic working. Whereas Wordsworth, and other poets like him, will too often not be content to allow us just to observe as we will, and to gain from our observation results which are no doubt limited by our capacities, but are at least our own; we must observe just in the way in which *they* want us to observe, and draw the conclusions which *they* want us to draw. The trouble with Wordsworth in this mood is not that he puts his hand in his breeches pocket but that he puts it all too firmly in our buttonholes. But the true poetry to Keats, as he read it, and with very few exceptions as he wrote it, is removed as far as may be from this assertive pedagogy. 'Man should not dispute or assert but whisper results to his neighbour and thus'—and then he launches out on a vision of the power of the interaction between human minds of which this great and unobtrusive poetry is part.

Keats' Craftsmanship, 1933 (p.8)

F. R. LEAVIS

To show from the Letters that 'Beauty' became for Keats a very subtle and embracing concept, and that in his use the term takes on meanings that it could not possibly have for the uninitiated, is gratuitous and irrelevant. However his use of the term may have developed as he matured, 'beauty' is the term he used; and in calling what seemed to him the supreme thing in life 'beauty,' he expressed a given bent—the bent everywhere manifested in the quality of his verse, in its 'loveliness.' His concern for beauty meant, at any rate in the first place, a concentration upon the purely delightful in experience to the exclusion of 'disagreeables.' And that 'beauty' in the *Ode on a Grecian Urn* expresses this bent is plain—that it should is the essence of the poem, and there is nothing in the poem to suggest otherwise.

When, then, the devotees of Art and Beauty later in the century made creedal or liturgical use of Keats's

'Beauty is truth, truth beauty,'

they were not falsifying its spirit (though it is one thing for him to say it, another thing for them to say it after him). They had at any rate gone the way it pointed, and it is worth while recalling briefly where they arrived. The pre-Raphaelite cult of Beauty, which developed into the religion of Art (or the aesthetic religiosity), is the completest expression of that Victorian romanticism which, in poetry, draws so much on the Keats of *The Eve of St. Agnes*, *The Eve of St. Mark* and *La Belle Dame sans Merci*. Victorian poetry in the central line that runs from the early Tennyson through Rossetti to Mr. Symons and his associates of the 'nineties turns its back on the actual world and preoccupies itself with fantasies of an alternative—in a spirit very different from Shelley's, for the Victorian poetic day-dream does not suppose itself to have any serious relation to actuality or possibility. . . . [Keats's aestheticism] does not mean any such cutting off of the special valued order of experience from direct, vulgar living ('Live!—our servants will do that for us') as is implied in the aesthetic antithesis of Art and Life.

Nevertheless, a certain drawing of frontiers, a wilful de-limitation of the 'true' or 'real' in experience, a focussing of the vision so as to shut out the uncongenial, is essentially the purpose of Keats's worship of Beauty—a purpose such as, uncountered and persisted in, must, we feel, necessarily result in devitalization. Actually, we feel also that there is in the poetry of this Keats, in the very richness and vitality with which he renders his 'exquisite sense of the luxurious,' an inherent contradiction: so strong a grasping at fulness of life implies a constitution, a being, that could not permanently refuse completeness of living.

* * *

If, then, in Keats's development from *Endymion* to the Ode *To Autumn* we see, as we may (leaving aside for a moment the *Hyperions*), the promise of greatness, it does not lie in any effective presence of the kind of seriousness aspired to in *Sleep and Poetry*:

> And can I ever bid these joys farewell?
> Yes, I must pass them for a nobler life,
> Where I may find the agonies, the strife
> Of human hearts . . .

It lies rather in the marvellous vitality of the art that celebrates 'these joys'—in the perfection attained within a limiting aestheticism. Remarkable intelligence and character are implied in that attainment, especially when we consider the starting-point and the surrounding influences: the beginning in 'pleasant smotherings,' with, as the incitement towards discipline, such poetic models as are represented by Leigh Hunt and the Cockney taste (at the highest level:

> Spenserian vowels that elope with ease
> And float along like birds o'er summer seas).

The achieved art itself, as has been argued, implies paradoxically, in the consummately kept limits of its perfection, something more serious than mere aestheticism.

'Keats', *Scrutiny*, March 1936 (pp.376–400).
Revaluation, 1936 (pp.254–65 *passim*)

G. WILSON KNIGHT

[Keats's] creative method can be partly defined in terms of his wide range of sensory perception. Visual imagery is not over-emphasized, with a corresponding flatness of result, but rather you tend to touch, to smell, to taste, to feel the living

217

warmth of one object after another. And yet none of these sense-impressions are direct: they are rather our own critical abstraction from a more complex whole. Keats writes with a feeling for an object which makes us aware of its weight or smoothness or warmth without any too direct assertion on his part: there is always more than the one simple appeal. He is continually losing himself in one whole of experience after another. With this reservation we can point to a valuable distinction. He does not offer much that is unpleasing to the tactile sense: the jagged or rough plays small part. Hence our awareness of the dome-like throughout a poetry largely concerned with nature, and of the smooth in statement however painful the emotions employed. His use of smell is most varied and subtle, contrasting with Shelley's less-realized 'odours.' The sensory suggestion is mostly pleasant. Closely allied is his almost excessive, and indeed at the first not always so subtle, use of taste.

The Starlit Dome, 1941 (pp.258–9)

LIONEL TRILLING

. . . we cannot think of Keats as a man without thinking of him in his occupation of poet. At the same time, when once we have read his letters, we cannot help knowing that his being a poet was his chosen way of being a man. . . . Keats was situated in a small way of life, that of the respectable, liberal, intellectual middle part of the middle class; . . . He nevertheless at every moment took life in the largest possible way and seems never to have been without the sense that to be, or to become, a man was an adventurous problem. The phrase in his letters that everyone knows, 'life is a vale of soul-making,' is his summing up of that sense, which, once we have become aware of its existence in him, we understand to have dominated his mind. He believed that life was given for him to find the right use of it, that it was a kind of continuous magical confrontation requiring to be met with the right answer.

'Introduction,' *Selected Letters of John Keats*, ed. L. Kronenberger, Farrar, Straus & Young, 1951. Reprinted in *The Opposing Self*, Secker & Warburg, 1955 (p.4)

Bibliography

Volumes Published in Keats's Lifetime

Poems (C. & J. Ollier, 1817).
Endymion: A Poetic Romance (Taylor and Hessey, 1818).
Lamia, Isabella, The Eve of St. Agnes, and Other Poems (Taylor and Hessey, 1820).

Editions and Works of Reference

Life, Letters, and Literary Remains, of John Keats, ed. Richard Monckton Milnes, 2 vols. (Edward Moxon, 1848). This biography is composed, largely, of a collection of Keats's letters and poems which Milnes (later Lord Houghton) was able to gather from Keats's friends. The work established a correct idea of Keats's character. It is in part available in Everyman's Library (1927) and World's Classics (1931).
Poetical Works and Other Writings of John Keats, ed. H. Buxton Forman, 4 vols. (Reeves & Turner, 1883). The *Library Edition* of Keats's writings with supplementary material. A supplementary volume appeared in 1890.
The Complete Works of John Keats, ed. H. Buxton Forman, 5 vols. (Gowans & Gray, 1900-1). The poems and Letters. Based on the *Library Edition*. Revised by M. Buxton Forman (Charles Scribner's Sons, 1938-9).
The Complete Poetical Works of John Keats, ed. H. Buxton Forman (Oxford University Press, 1907, frequently reprinted).
The Poems of John Keats, ed. E. De Sélincourt (Methuen, 1905, frequently revised and reprinted). Complete poetry with copious notes.
The Poetical Works of John Keats, ed. H. W. Garrod (Oxford University Press, 1939, 1958). The definitive edition, with full critical apparatus.

BIBLIOGRAPHY

The Letters of John Keats, ed. M. Buxton Forman, 2 vols. (Oxford University Press, 1931; 2nd edn. in 1 vol. 1935, reprinted).

The Letters of John Keats, 1814-21, ed. H. E. Rollins, 2 vols. (Harvard University Press, 1958). The definitive edition of the Letters.

ROLLINS, HYDER EDWARD (ed.), *The Keats Circle*, 2 vols. (Harvard University Press, Oxford University Press, 1948). Letters and papers giving information about Keats, his family and friends, and about Milnes and his biography. Most of the material comes from the Houghton Library at Harvard University.

BALDWIN, D. L. (et al.), *A Concordance of the Poems of John Keats* (Carnegie Institute, 1917).

MACGILLIVRAY, J. R., *Keats: A Bibliography and Reference Guide* (University of Toronto Press, 1949). A meticulously compiled bibliography covering all aspects of Keats studies. There is a good essay on Keats's reputation.

ROSSETTI, W. M., *Life of John Keats* (Walter Scott, *Great Writers Series*, 1887). William Michael is not as sympathetic with his subject as Dante Gabriel would have been.

COLVIN, SIR SIDNEY, *John Keats: His Life and Poetry, His Friends, Critics and After-Fame* (Macmillan, 1917, 1918, 1920). A full biographical and critical account of Keats. The best large-scale biography.

LOWELL, AMY, *John Keats*, 2 vols. (Jonathan Cape, 1925). This biography presents material not in Colvin's work, but lacks his discernment.

BATE, WALTER JACKSON, *John Keats* (Harvard University Press, Oxford University Press, 1963). A large-scale study of Keats's life and work, incorporating the results of recent research.

Criticism

(1) *Recommended for use in schools and universities*

COLVIN, SIR SIDNEY, *Keats* (Macmillan, 1887, *English Men of Letters Series*, frequently reprinted in various editions). A short penetrating study of Keats's life and work.

MAYHEAD, R., *Keats* (Cambridge University Press, 1967).

(2) Recommended more particularly for university students

FORD, G. H., *Keats and the Victorians* (Yale University Press, Oxford University Press, 1944). Traces the influences of Keats on the Victorian poets.

ARNOLD, MATTHEW, 'John Keats,' *The English Poets*, ed. T. H. Ward (Macmillan, 1880), Vol. IV, pp. 427-37. Reprinted in *Essays in Criticism, Second Series* (Macmillan, 1888), pp. 100-21. An important critical essay on Keats.

BRIDGES, ROBERT, *John Keats, A Critical Essay* (Privately printed, 1895). An influential essay which was printed as an introduction to G. Thorn Drury's *Poems of John Keats* (Lawrence & Bullen, 1896), and in Bridges' *Collected Essays*, Vol. IV (Oxford University Press, 1929).

GARROD, H. W., *Keats* (Oxford University Press, 1926, rev. 1939). A short, penetrating critical study by a prominent Keats scholar.

MURRY, JOHN MIDDLETON, *Keats and Shakespeare* (Oxford University Press, 1925). Critical essays on Keats. Murry's opinions are sometimes extravagant, but he is often stimulating.

MURRY, JOHN MIDDLETON, *Studies in Keats* (Oxford University Press, 1930). To subsequent editions, new essays were added, and the volume published under a new title: *Studies in Keats: New and Old* (1939), *The Mystery of Keats* (1949), *Keats* (Jonathan Cape, 1955).

RIDLEY, M. R., *Keats' Craftsmanship* (Oxford University Press, 1933). In discussing Keats's methods of composition makes a detailed and lively study of nearly all the *Poems of 1820*. A valuable work of criticism.

LEAVIS, F. R., 'Keats,' *Scrutiny*, March 1936, pp. 376-400. Reprinted in *Revaluation* (Chatto & Windus, 1936), pp. 241-73. An important critical essay with some emphasis on *Ode to a Nightingale* and *The Fall of Hyperion*.

ELIOT, T. S., *The Use of Poetry and the Use of Criticism* (Harvard University Press, 1933), pp. 78-94.

BATE, WALTER JACKSON, *Negative Capability* (Harvard University Press, 1939). A short study of the 'intuitive approach in Keats' by a prominent scholar.

KNIGHT, G. WILSON, *The Starlit Dome* (Oxford University

Press, 1941), pp. 258-307. A discerning study of Keats's imagery.

BROOKS, CLEANTH, 'History without Footnotes: An Account of Keats' Urn,' *Sewanee Review*, 52 (1944), pp. 89-101. Reprinted in *The Well Wrought Urn* (Dennis Dobson, 1949, and University Paperbacks, Methuen, 1968). A detailed study of Keats's ode.

WASSERMAN, E. R., *The Finer Tone* (Johns Hopkins Press, 1953). Critical studies of *Ode on a Grecian Urn, Ode to a Nightingale, The Eve of St. Agnes, Lamia, La Belle Dame sans Merci*.

GITTINGS, ROBERT, *The Living Year* (Heinemann, 1954). A detailed, sometimes conjectural, account of the events in Keats's life from 21 September 1818 to 21 September 1819.

(3) *Recommended for advanced university students*

THORPE, C. D., *The Mind of John Keats* (Oxford University Press, 1926). Gathers together material that bears on Keats's aesthetic and philosophic thought.

FINNEY, C. L., *The Evolution of Keats's Poetry*, 2 vols. (Harvard University Press, 1936). Copiously relates Keats's poetry to the events of his life and to its sources in his reading.

MUIR, KENNETH (ed.), *John Keats: A Reassessment* (Liverpool University Press, 1958). Critical essays by various hands, demonstrating the conflict in Keats between the attraction of the world of beauty and the world of reality.

Index of Titles

Index of First Lines